Library of Congress
Cataloging-in-Publication Data

Way Inside ESPN's X Games—1st. ed.
  p. cm.
  ISBN 0-7868-8292-1
  1. ESPN X Games
  I. ESPN (tv network)
GV722.5.E76W39 1998
796—dc21   98-15103
          CIP

Editorial Director
Shelley Youngblut

Art Director
Helene Silverman/Hello Studio

Designer
Heidi Fener

Writer
Kevin Brooker

Associate Editor
Jenny Ford

Copy Editor
Felicity Stone

Photo Editor
Hadas Dembo

Feature Photography
Michael Wong

Action Photography
Eric Lars Bakke
Scott Clarke
Dana Paul

Assistant Editor
Monica Schroer

FIRST EDITION
10 9 8 7 6 5 4 3 2 1

WAY INSIDE ESPN'S X GAMES

HYPERION
ESPN
BOOKS

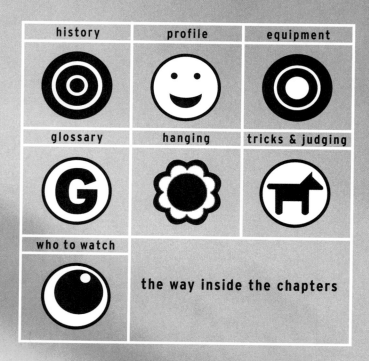

history	profile	equipment
glossary	hanging	tricks & judging
who to watch	the way inside the chapters	

INTRODUCTION

BY KEVIN BROOKER

EVERYTHING OLD SCHOOL IS NEW SCHOOL AGAIN

As much fun as the classical Greeks had inventing civilization and then enslaving everyone else in the name of it, things must have gotten boring after a while. How else can you explain the bizarre scenes of buff young Cretans kickin' it with their homies found painted on items of ancient pottery.

It seems that a young Greek would run full-speed at a snarling bull, dive at its head, grasp the horns and sprock a front somersault over the startled animal's back. The details are not clear. Was it a judged event, or just showing off? If style was an issue, did distance count? Would the better bulls have "Demetri's Extra-Round Chariot Wheels" branded on their flanks?

We don't know these things, but we do know this: If some of the oldest art on the planet depicts people doing insane stuff just for kicks, it's safe to assume that Generation X didn't invent it. Humans have apparently had the art of survival dialed for so long, they spent the last several thousand years thinking up wack new ways to put it to the test. They've been hucking themselves absurdly, racing obsessively and stunting foolishly ever since monkeyhood.

SIX DEGREES OF SURFING

Along the Darwinian march, people increasingly used technology to take thrill-seeking to sophisticated new levels. Before long, Micronesian islanders were bungeeing with vines tied to their ankles. Vikings strapped boards on their feet and raced around frozen Scandinavia. With the dawn of the Industrial Age, it was cannon shots, tightropes, wing-walking, Niagara Falls in a barrel.

But if you want to identify the one historical variant that most influences the anarchic sports culture of the late 20th century, it has to be the ancient Hawaiian sport of surfing. In a spirit now shared with every event at the X Games, those Polynesian kings had it figured out centuries ago: They took a simple piece of equipment, a little lateral thinking and suddenly, they turned an inhospitable element into a pulse-pounding playground. They also invented attitude as we know it today, by endowing the sport with religious overtones while reserving the primo breaks and da kine boards for themselves. Presto, instant cult.

It was Americans who re-embraced surfing in the early part of this century. In California, while Dutch Reagan and his cronies butted leather helmets, refugees from the gridiron headed for the beach and discovered the primal buzz of connecting a healthy body with the oceanic soul. Most importantly, they became madly addicted to an activity that

almost nobody in mainstream society knew or understood. And they liked it that way.

"We're all surfers," says street luger Biker Sherlock of his X Games colleagues. He doesn't just mean that they all add wave-riding to their adrenaline diet—though many, of course, do—he means that the way X Gamers move through ordinary environments duplicates the surfer's mode of carving out his own highly personalized amusement.

Take skateboarding. Ironically, the urban rats who invented skateboarding as we know it did not want to skateboard. They wanted to surf. A chunk of plywood rigged up with rollerskate parts was intended only to be a time-killer, a lame proxy to take one's mind off the tragic absence of swell when the Pacific lived up to its name.

It did not take them long, however, to realize that waves are only a sometime thing, and at their best last only a few seconds each. Those protopunks would have grasped immediately that a skateboard's ride never ends, making it the perfect accessory in a California where it was plain to see that the paving thing was not about to go away. Mankind had had a nice run with upright posture and bipedal locomotion, but let's face it: walking bites. It's so . . . pedestrian. With a skateboard, on the other opposable-thumbed hand, you can go wherever you want and all the while appear to be *just standing there*. Styling.

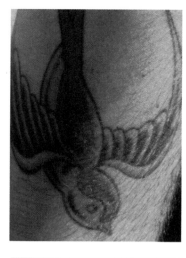

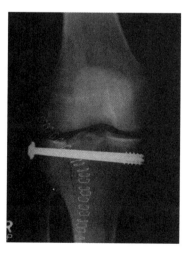

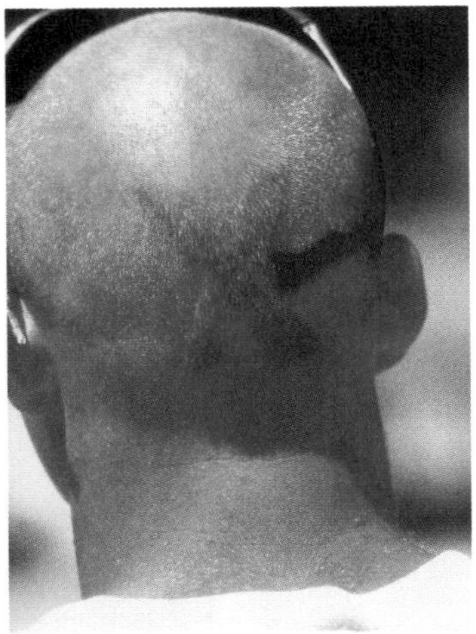

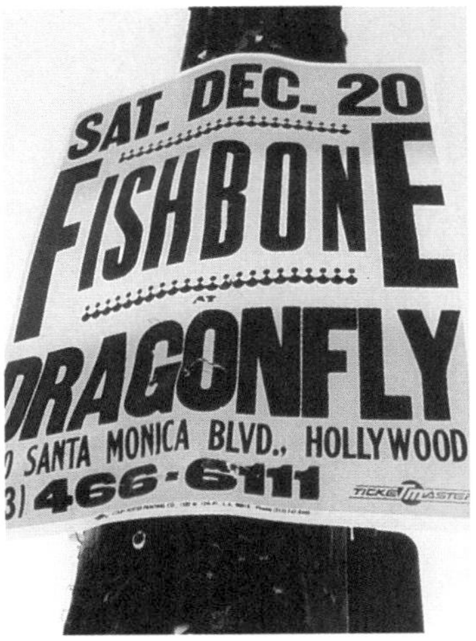
SAT. DEC. 20
FISHBONE
AT
DRAGONFLY
SANTA MONICA BLVD., HOLLYWOOD
466-6111

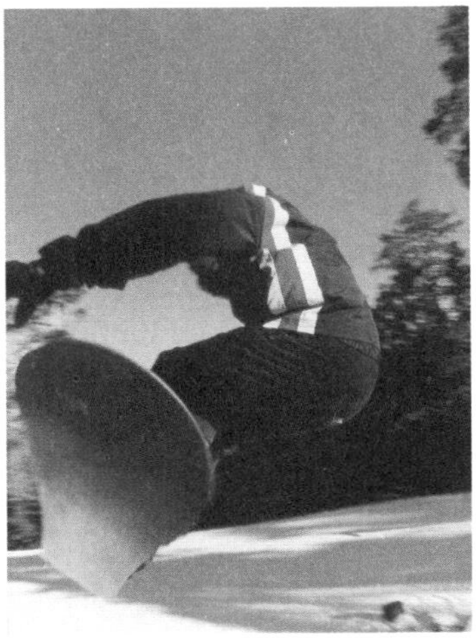

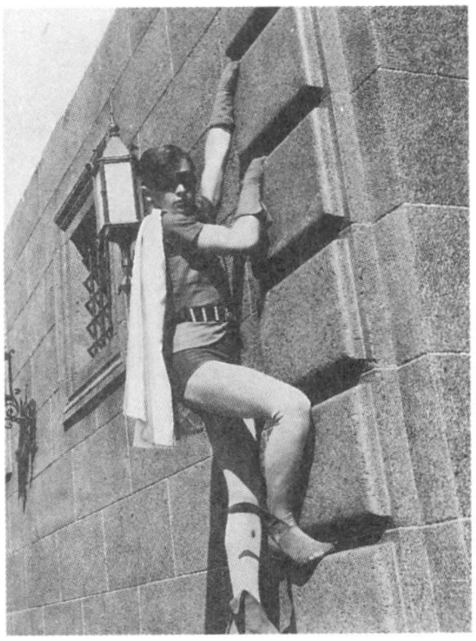

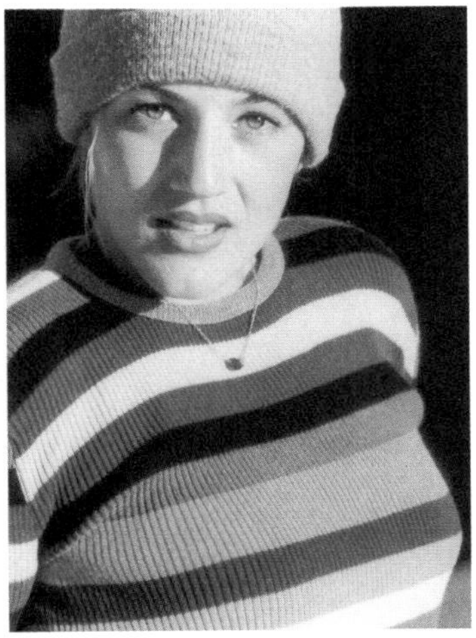

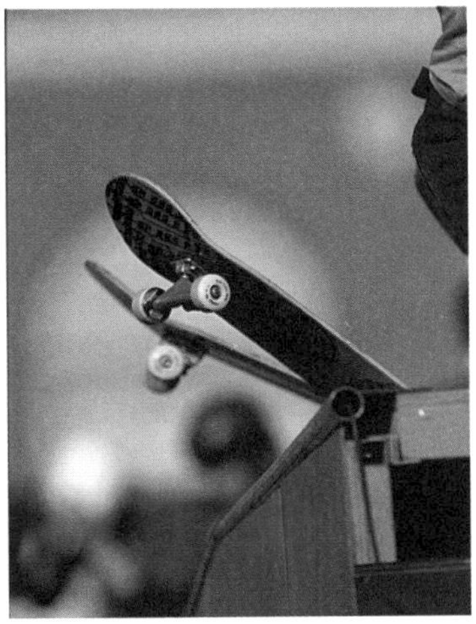

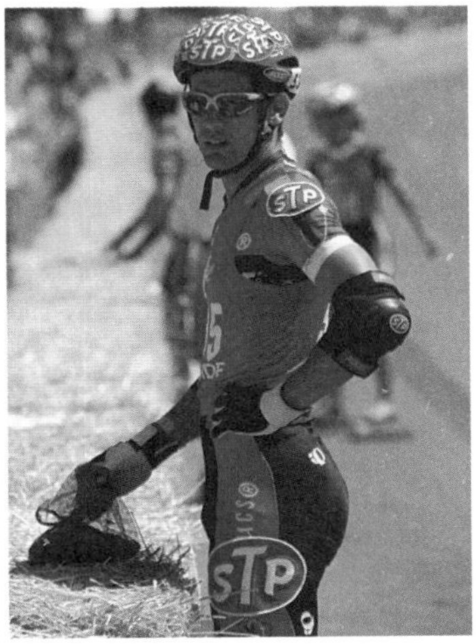
STP
STP

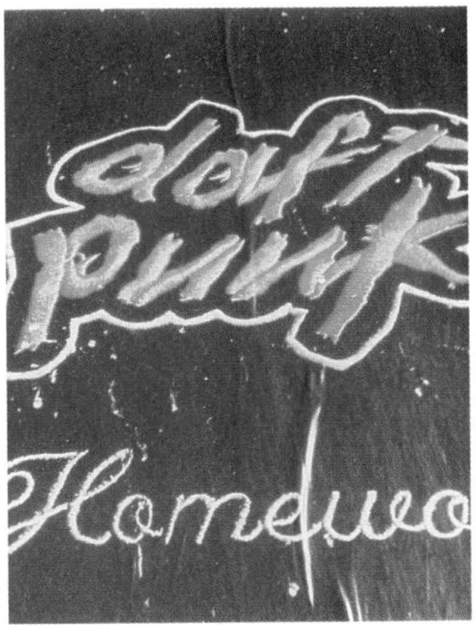
daft punk
Homewo

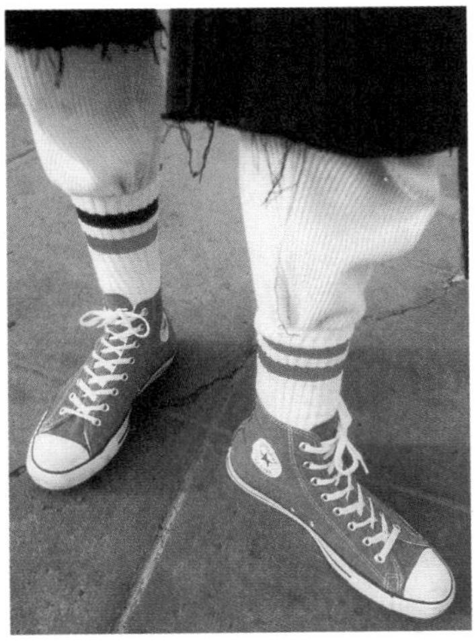

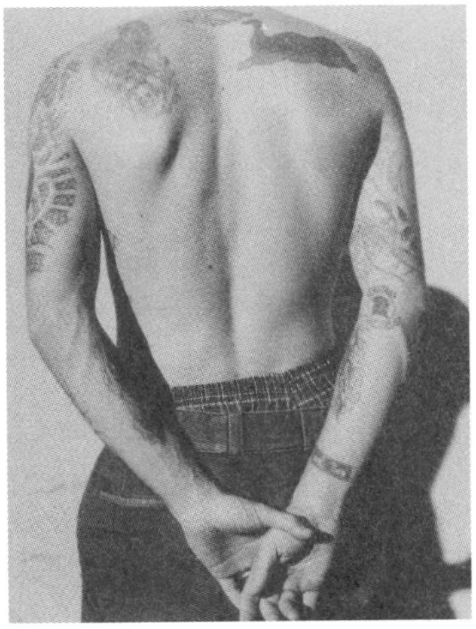

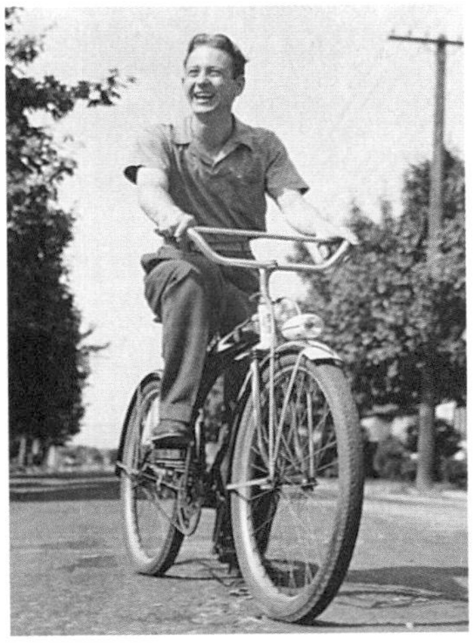

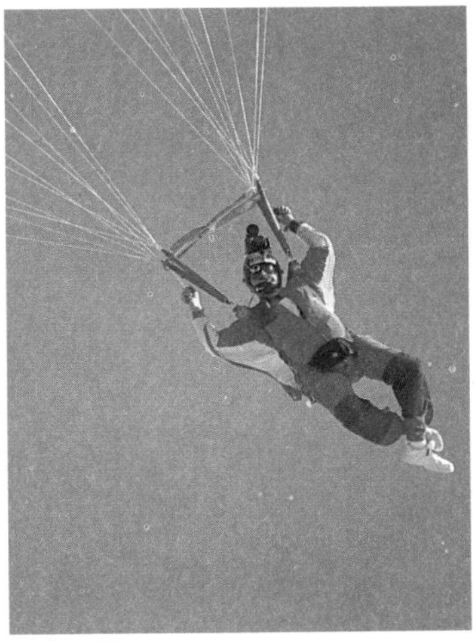

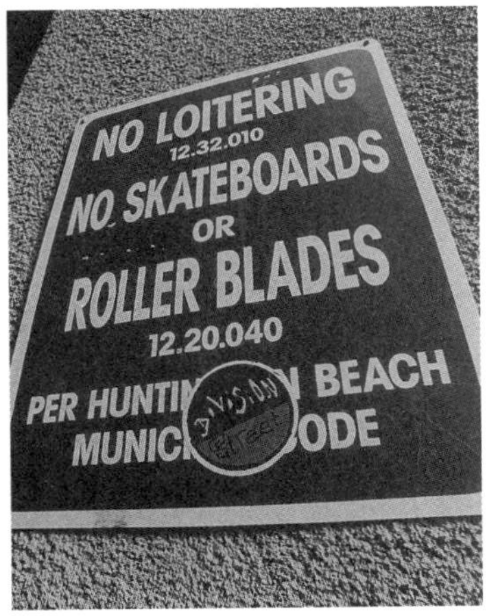
NO LOITERING
12.32.010
NO SKATEBOARDS
OR
ROLLER BLADES
12.20.040
PER HUNTIN BEACH
MUNIC ODE

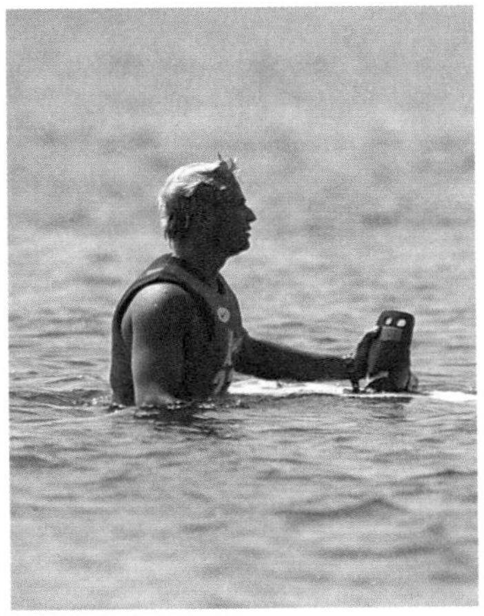

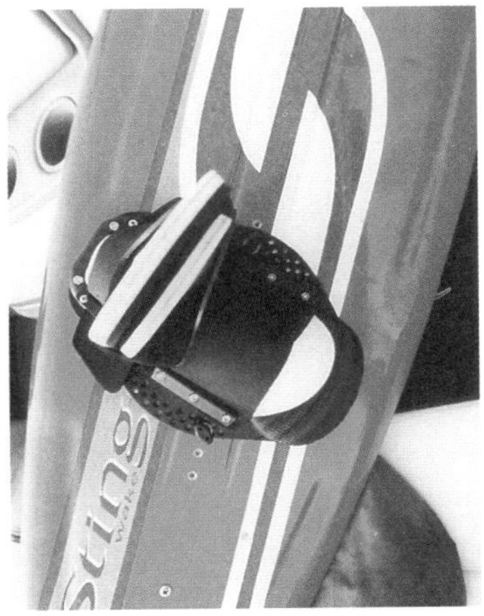
Sting

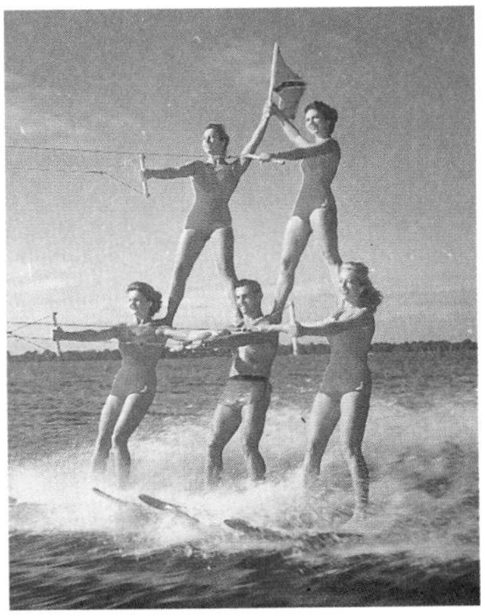

From then on skateboarding did not spend one second being uncool. And while, as a fad, it may have waned periodically, it never would, or could, go away. Whether used as a toy in a private soul session or as a symbolic, double-axled cross held up against the hypocrisy of town elders, the magic board lays tracks of cool across what would otherwise be an arid concrete wasteland.

Thus, the roots of what is now celebrated in the X Games began to spread out. Skateboarding begat snowboarding, street luge, skysurfing and wakeboarding. It challenged in-liners and stunt bikers to master its terrain. Off in their own worlds, sportclimbers and barefoot jumpers could now look at the exploding alternative sports scene and declare, in spite of their own dangerous idiosyncrasies, that, hey, we're a legit tribe too.

What unified them was an attitude at once reckless and super-controlled, a daring approach that came to be known as extreme. The word itself entered common sports parlance from French, in the 1970s, when Patrick Vallençant and Sylvain Saudan referred to their conquest of Chamonix couloirs as *ski extrème*.

Translated to English, it served for a long time as a useful description for any activity that appeared to go, as the dictionary says, "far beyond the bounds of moderation; exceeding what is considered reasonable; radical."

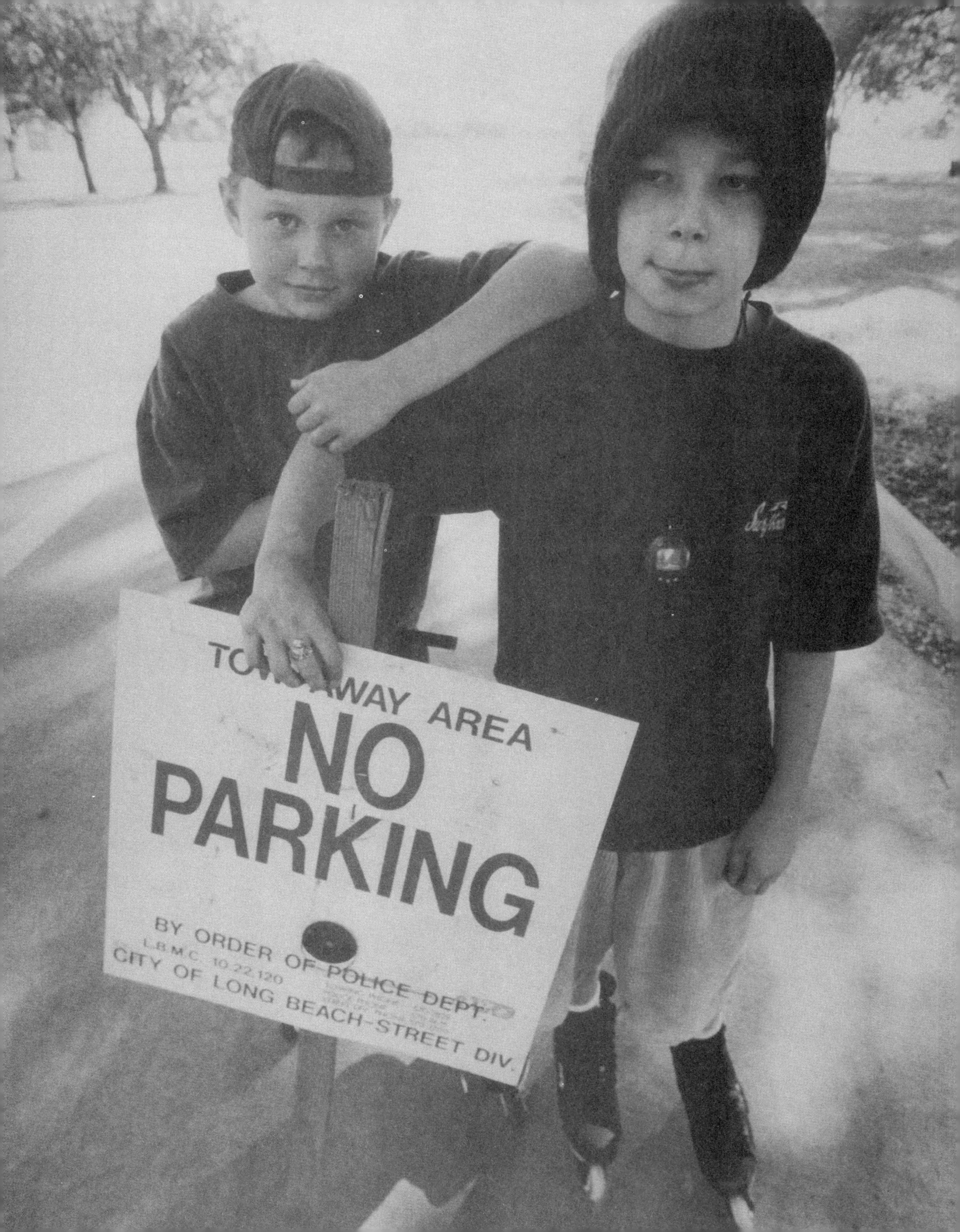
AWAY AREA
NO PARKING
BY ORDER OF POLICE DEPT.
L.B.M.C. 10.22.120
CITY OF LONG BEACH-STREET DIV.

WHY JASON DON'T PLAY SHORTSTOP

Once it had migrated throughout the sports world to every activity north of bowling on the thrill scale, extreme lost its strength as a concept. By another definition, the word means "situated at the farthest limit; outermost." Logically, the more often it is employed, the less likely it can really be the case. Extreme now means little more than "something that was deemed cool and difficult in 1988 but now just looks weak."

Still, like a genie that can't be put back in the bottle, extremism—or whatever you want to call it—stalks the land. A combination of extraordinary individual achievement and unmatched personal enjoyment makes for a potent beverage. For those who have sipped from it, there is no turning back to the primitive, hierarchical games of the past. Baseball's fine, for example, but when you take out the poetry and the smell of a well-worn glove and your beloved old card collection, what are you left with? A loser factory, where only a minuscule percentage of players have a hope of securing a spot in The Show, and all the rest are spat joylessly out of the system. If you do not show "talent" somewhere "early" in your development—in other words, if you are not six foot two with a full beard by the age of eight—forget it. That's the end of the deal. Look around: do you see anyone playing hardball for fun anymore? Not to mention women, who were never invited in the first place.

No wonder the corner sandlot is history, while kids are turning by the thousands to activities where their feats are measured in terms of their own stoke rather than Coach Squarejaw's approval. Jason and Jenny are now hanging blissfully at the skatepark or the lake or the climbing wall, where nobody gets chewed out and no referee's whistle shatters the peace.

Sometimes Mom and Dad understand it. At other times, they're just plain mystified: after all, these kids are supposed to be slackers, but they're devoting 10-hour days to these damn hobbies.

Fortunately, exposure to the likes of the X Games helps make sense of this lifestyle to the uninitiated. Not that anyone is going to lose sleep if America fails to dig it. Sure, it's nice to eke out a living doing what you love most, but what's more important is to eke out a life, period.

The X Games have been criticized as a "made-for-TV event." (Yeah, like the Super Bowl is all for the benefit of the folks in the stands.) But what makes this substantially different is that these athletes would be doing all of this anyway. The X Games merely offer a simple proposition: Girlfriend, you wanna show what you got? Here are state-of-the-art cameras—bring it on.

Cancer will not be cured. Peace may not break out. But at the very least, a worldwide audience will learn that young people today are not going to hell in a handcart—they're going to heaven on a street luge. You are invited to ride shotgun. Please sign all appropriate releases.

SKATEBOARDING

STYLE. AGGRESSION. UNCANNY TRICKS. HEROIC PANTS.

Skateboarding is the spiritual Kali of the X Games, the mother of all sick airs, scabs on scabs and truly stupid devotion to precise body control. Too numerous to be a cult, less cohesive than a tribe, skateboarders are nonetheless unified by the certain knowledge that being three inches above the pavement is a better way to hang. Bylaw enforcers everywhere tried to ban it but instead managed only to send skateboarding happily, defiantly underground. It lurks there still, from Helsinki to Houston, smoldering like a fire in a coal mine. At the X Games, the flames rise considerably above the surface.

No single piece of equipment sums up the X Games attitude quite like a skateboard. Part prop, part vehicle and all sex symbol, a hard-worn deck has become such a potent talisman of cool that a vast army of young people wouldn't dream of entering adolescence without it.

1940s Kids start using broken scooters as skateboards. Steel wheels are standard. They suck, but at least they make riding more dangerous so it's cool. **1959** The square-nosed Roller Derby Skateboard, $9.95, hits stores. Primitive trucks and clay wheels, which also suck, are now standard. **1963** Makaha makes first surf-inspired skateboard. First skateboarding competition, Pier Avenue Junior High School in Hermosa Beach, CA. Vert invented in Gary Swanson's Santa Monica backyard, the world's first pool session. **1964** Hobie introduces fiberglass skateboard. First issue of *SkateBoarder*. Jim Fitzpatrick takes skateboarding to Europe. Chicago Roller Skating Co. introduces the nylon wheel. Still sucks. Jan and Dean record "Sidewalk Surfin'" (includes sounds of actual skateboarding). By year end, 92 skateboard manufacturers sell future collector's items priced from $1.79 to $49.95 for a "Tiger Skate." **1965** The first international skateboarding competition–freestyle and slalom on a huge, purpose-built ramp–at Anaheim's La Palma Stadium, and it's covered by all three TV networks. Sport's first movie (an art film, really) is Noel Black's *Skater-Dater*–it wins Academy Award for Best Documentary. Then, safety experts pronounce skateboarding dangerous, town councils freak out and the sport enters its first Dark Age. **1969** Hardcores persist. Makaha's Larry Stevenson is awarded the patent for the kicktail. **1973** Finally, a wheel that doesn't suck: Frank Nasworthy flogs urethane wheels under the brand name Cadillac. Bennett starts making the most popular truck of the '70s. Grip tape introduced. The modern age has begun. **1975** Manufacturers begin sponsoring pros like Jay Adams and Stacy Peralta. Tony Alva defines the DogTown style (aka, Santa Monica, where skateboarding never died): angry hair, flying out of the pool, anti-mellow. Elsewhere, knee socks are thought to be cool. Larry Balma invents Tracker Trucks. First Doubles event at Orange County's "Big O" competition. **1976** The first smooth-concrete ("gunite") skatepark opens in Carlsbad, CA. Across the U.S., 132 parks follow suit and vertical skating sweeps the nation. George Orton takes aerial moves to a new level. **1977** Bobby Valdez does the first inverted hand plant. Movie *Skateboard* released; does not win Academy Award. **1978** Alan "Ollie" Gelfand invents the move that makes it possible to catch air without grabbing the board. Armed now with its core trick, street skating gathers steam. Insurance hassles force skateparks to close. **1980** Skaters start building plywood ramps at the home of the one set of cool parents on the block. Serious hanging begins. **1981** *SkateBoarder* publishes its last issue. Skating is driven even further underground, where it meets punk. Adults still think it will "go away." **1982** Despite *No Skateboarding* signs everywhere, street skating rules. The Rusty Harris Series begins, then turns into the National Skateboard

Association. Fourteen-year-old Tony Hawk wins first state contest at Delmar State Ranch. *Thrasher* begins publication. **1983** New contest format for Vert contests introduced at Joe's Ramp Jam. *Transworld Skateboarding* begins publication. **1984** *The Bones Brigade* video premieres, auguring a jerky, hand-held aesthetic that will reign for centuries. "Skatepunk" is now an official school clique across North America. **1986** The Transworld Skateboarding Championships are held at the World's Fair in Vancouver, B.C. Animal Chin, the first multi-faceted ramp, is built for a Powell video. **1987** *Poweredge* begins publication. **1990** Roger Hickey sets speed records of 78.37 mph in the prone position and 55.43 mph upright. Tony Hawk is named Skater of the Decade by *Thrasher*. Cara-Beth Burnside becomes first female pro since ancient knee sock times. **1991** National Skateboarding Association (NSA) runs competitions in Germany, Spain, France and the U.S. **1992** *Big Brother* begins publication. **1994** The NSA folds. Contests continue without sanctioning body. **1995** World Cup Skateboarding becomes leading contest organizer. ESPN's summer X Games launch in Newport, RI. **1996** Skateboarding joins bicycle stunt and aggressive in-line for a multi-site assault across the country, including the Olympics opening ceremonies in Atlanta. ESPN's second X Games take place in Newport, RI. **1997** The first signature trucks—the Tony Hawk pro model—produced by Tracker Trucks. ESPN's X Games move to San Diego. Nike unveils ad campaign asking, "What if we treated tennis players like skateboarders?"

ACID DROP Riding straight off an obstacle and free-falling to the ground. **CABALLERIAL** Named for the legendary Steve Caballero, it's riding fakie to air 360 degrees with no grab, then back down the ramp riding regular. A *Half Cab* is a 180. **CROOKED GRIND** Front axle and nose scrape the coping together. Also, *K.* **DISASTER** A lip trick in which you get hung up on the coping, usually with the board perpendicular. **FEEBLE GRIND** Back truck and toe-side rail both grind. **FIFTY-FIFTY** Both trucks are grinding. If it's just the back, it's a *Five-O*. **HAND PLANT** Any trick where you slap a paw onto the coping. **HEELFLIP** Putting pressure on the heels while ollying, which causes the board to flip before landing. **KICKFLIP** Like a *Heelflip*, only the toes do all the work. **LIPSLIDE** Tail slides laterally on the coping. **MANUAL** Another name for a *Wheelie*. *Nose Manual* if it's up front. **MCTWIST** A 540 spin with a grab, named for Mike McGill. **OLLIE** The building block of modern street skating, it's a no-handed tail-tap jump sequence that sends both board and rider into the air. With a nose tap, it's a *Nollie*. **RAILSLIDE** To slide on an obstacle or coping on the underside of the deck. Also *Noseslide* and *Tailslide*. **ROCK AND ROLL** Tapping the underside of the board on the coping, then doing a Kick Turn. **SHOVE IT** A trick involving spinning the board horizontally 180 degrees without changing stance or direction. **STALEFISH AIR** A frontside trick in which the rear hand grabs the back edge while the front leg is boned. **VARIAL** Shoving it during an aerial. **WALLRIDE** To ride on a wall that has no transition by ollying up and then ollying off before the momentum dies.

Tricks are at the core of competition riding. Skateboarding itself was born in the street where you learn a trick just to prove to yourself it can be done. After that, it's all about showing off. Judges want to see tricks that are big, burly and, above all, like you ain't even breaking a sweat. Airs should be huge, grabs stylish and flailing at any time will be penalized by low scores and surefire heckling. Work as much of the terrain as possible, be creative, link smoothly.

Skateboarding's colorful vocabulary leads many rampsiders to think it necessary to carry an English-Thrashing dictionary. But for the most part, don't sweat it. Any trick or tech term, given the sport's patterns of ruthless invention, parallel evolution and even I'll-change-it-as-soon-as-you-learn-it bloody-mindedness, will take on multiple identities. Some of these expressions have the staying power of words like "bat" and "ball" in other sports, and may well dangle from the lips of X Games anchors in the future. However, if all these terms remain unchanged and are not joined by several hundred other skanky neologisms, turn off the TV: you're watching lawn bowling.

ALLEY-OOP A trick performed in the opposite direction to which the skater is moving. However, in today's leg-boning, 10-tricks-per-second competition world, it's really hard to tell. BACKSIDE For a regular, left-foot-forward rider, it's a clockwise turn. Abbreviated as *b/s* (*f/s* for *frontside*), it's a fundamental factor in trick difficulty and is therefore usually specified. BLUNT Any trick that includes tail- or nose-first contact. CARVE To make a long, curving turn while skating. For old dudes. COPING A rounded lip at the top of the ramp or obstacle, usually made of metal, cement or PVC pipe. If it's too small to grind properly, it's called *ghetto coping.* FAKIE Backwards, as in keeping the stance the same but riding fakie. Not to be confused with riding *switch* (see below). GOOFY Riding with the right foot forward. You ride *regular* if the left foot is forward. HANG UP When either truck catches on an obstacle, usually resulting in a fall. HIP The spot where a ramp or obstacle comes to a point. KICK TURN A trick in which pressure is applied to the tail of the board, lifting the front, which is then redirected. KNEE SLIDE A way of controlling a fall by sliding on the plastic caps of knee pads. LIP The upper edge of a ramp or obstacle. RUN A series of tricks in a sequence. SWITCH SIDING Riding *goofy* if you normally ride *regular*. One of the hardest things in skateboarding to do well, top pros are still only approaching total ambidexterity. TRANSITION The part of a ramp where two angles are joined, usually a curve that connects horizontal and vertical.

THE FIRST TRULY VERTICAL SKATING TOOK PLACE in the 1970s, with skaters shredding empty California swimming pools that featured smoothly curved concrete walls. Later, some skateboarders discovered segments of giant sewer mains yet to be installed underground and showed the world what thrills awaited it in the form of pipe riding. Modern ramp skating owes a little to both developments. It combines the smoothness and predictable geometry of a pipe, the rounded coping of a swimming pool and the sense of skaters egging one another on as they session ultra-radical terrain.

At the X Games, the six Vert judges are a little like the posse of onlookers waiting their turn in the pool. They want to see skaters max out their vertical, add heaps of personal style, land all their tricks smoothly and throw in one or two never-before-seen moves just to up the ante. Over the years, various systems have been tried in order to codify the judging, but because of intangibles, they seldom work: there's really no replacement for the overall impression of expert skateboarders who know a huge run when they see it. Judges assign a whole-number score out of 100. The highest and lowest judgements are thrown out, leaving four scores that are then averaged. In Vert preliminary rounds, each skater gets two 50-second runs of which only the best score counts. The top 10 who reach the finals get three more runs. Again, if they score big on their first run, they can go for broke in subsequent ones because the best single score wins.

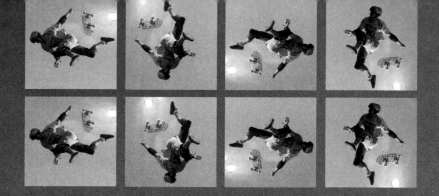

AROUND THE WORLD, STREET SKATING is the most popular form of skateboarding, if only because it's the one kind of riding most people have access to. Of course, everybody's streetscape is a little different, and, as some critics hasten to point out, none of them looks like the X Games' artificial garden of ramps, walls and obstacles. So what. Say what you will about the architecture, the X Games Street competition nevertheless adheres to street skating's core values: style your way around and across bizarre terrain in a skanky demonstration that the urban landscape is your personal playground.

That puts a premium on individual flair and creativity. The half-dozen judges each render a whole-number score out of 100, and you can bet it will go up if a skater makes a serious effort to use the terrain differently with each new run. And if, seemingly on the spur of the moment, he busts tricks that nobody saw him try even in warm-up, the street gods will be further appeased. On the other hand, no street skater helps his cause by sacrificing amplitude for smoothness, or appearing overly choreographed,

Like Vert, the preliminaries consist of two runs, of which the highest counts. The top 10 competitors then skate two one-minute runs in the final round. Since only one score matters, there's no excuse for holding back. Whining that this ain't real street terrain won't cut it.

1	2	3	4	5	6	7	8	9	10
11	12	13	14	15	16	17	18	19	20
21	22	23	24	25	26	27	28	29	30
31	32	33	34	35	36	37	38	39	40
41	42	43	44	45	46	47	48	49	50
51	52	53	54	55	56	57	58	59	60
61	62	63	64	65	66	67	68	69	70
71	72	73	74	75	76	77	78	79	80
81	82	83	84	85	86	87	88	89	90
91	92	93	94	95	96	97	98	99	100

1	2	3	4	5	6	7	8	9	10
11	12	13	14	15	16	17	18	19	20
21	22	23	24	25	26	27	28	29	30
31	32	33	34	35	36	37	38	39	40
41	42	43	44	45	46	47	48	49	50
51	52	53	54	55	56	57	58	59	60
61	62	63	64	65	66	67	68	69	70
71	72	73	74	75	76	77	78	79	80
81	82	83	84	85	86	87	88	89	90
91	92	93	94	95	96	97	98	99	100

NOT MANY SKATEBOARD COMPS FEATURE A DOUBLES EVENT, although its history extends well back to the 1970s. In part, Doubles was a communal response by skaters who were used to crowding into half-pipes, which were then, as now, in short supply. It also turned out to be an excellent way to showcase the ever-escalating precision of the sport, with co-ordinated tricks demonstrating that an entire run can be planned, as opposed to the notion that a skater just performs whatever tricks come chaotically to mind.

Like in ordinary solo Vert, the six X Games judges render impression-based scores from 1 to 100 focusing on originality, difficulty, flow, use of ramp, combination tricks and amplitude. Where they look for something different is in the interaction of the partners. Tricks intended to be simultaneous, for example, should not be rhythmically a half-beat off. Skaters flying above the coping should reach identical heights. And the pair should introduce risky elements such as crossovers. At the '97 X Games, for example, Tony Hawk and Andy Macdonald won the judges over with a solid repertoire of both matching and complementary tricks. Hawk executed a rare 720 over top while Macdonald did a Tailslide underneath. Macdonald also pulled two mid-air trade-offs, with Hawk dishing him his own deck and then another. In all, Macdonald rode three different boards during that run without once coming to a stop.

LIKE EVERYTHING ELSE IN SKATEBOARDING, there are no rules regarding board design, yet the basic setup of deck/wheels/trucks has been the same for over three decades. Variations in geometry, materials and specific details depend on specific use. Materials seem to be constant except for differences in hardness. **PRO DECKS** are generally laminated maple, 8 inches x 31 inches, covered in **GRIP TAPE**, kicked up at **NOSE** and **TAIL**, with a flex and concavity according to rider preference. Urethane **WHEELS** are measured by size and hardness. The larger the wheels, the faster they roll over surface imperfections. Softer wheels are good for recreational cruising and long boards. The harder they are, the better suited to Street and Vert competition. Wheel hardnesses are measured numerically by a durometer: 85A (soft), 90A (firm), 95A (extra firm), 97A and up (hard). Inside the wheel are **BEARINGS**, which can have a tighter or looser feel. **TRUCKS** flex due to urethane **BUSHINGS** in the **KING PIN**, whose hardnesses are also rated by a durometer. The firmer they are, the more stable but less turnable the truck. **RAMP BOARDS** have large, firm wheels with wide trucks for stability. Many skaters feel that more concavity allows better control in the air. **STREET BOARDS** are generally shorter and narrower with hard wheels. As ever, personal preference rules. **RAMPS** are made of two-by-four frames and layers of plywood covered with tempered **MASONITE**. At the top of the Vert wall, where it meets the platform, is a PVC pipe called **COPING**. Street courses often use wood and coping to simulate the concrete environment where skaters normally hang, in any combination of stairs, fun boxes, quarter-pipes, half-pipes, jumps and free-standing obstacles like rails. The only other gear you'll need is comfortable skateboard **SNEAKERS** with grippy rubber soles that extend far enough up the sides to enable superlative board-flipping control. Rumor has it that these may be purchased.

RUNE GLIFBERG Confident, fast, revolutionary. A master in all disciplines, this Dane leaves 'em speechless with his sick Stalefish Airs, Grinds and Disasters.

TONY HAWK Focused and relaxed atop the Vert world. One run in the half-pipe can combine technical lip tricks, lofty airs and incomprehensible spins and inverts. Hit four consecutive 540s, using a different grab on each, in his '97 gold medal performance.

ANDY MACDONALD This technical genius can blast large Fingerflips on one transition and long, deafening grinds on the other. Lives clean, skates hard.

CHRIS SENN The San Francisco Street magician is the last of a dying breed of hard-core skaters in a sport that some feel is becoming too commercial. Insanely talented, relentlessly anti-establishment.

BOB BURNQUIST The Brazilian has upped the ante in Vert and Street skating utilizing switch stance during every maneuver, electrifying crowds and fellow skaters with next-to-impossible Ollies, Grinds and Alley-oops.

CAINE GAYLE Laidback member of the DC shoes Droors posse known for big Kickflips, Railslides and Grinds to Disasters. Able to ollie gigantic gaps.

HAWK & MACDONALD (DOUBLES) Two of the world's best, killing it together: as the Hawk soars, Andy Mac grinds. Simultaneous 540s, board switches and board stalls make them the best in the world.

TONY HAWK

THAT THE MAN WHOM *THRASHER* NAMED SKATEBOARDER OF THE DECADE for the 1980s is even alive is amazing enough. That he still rules contests in 1998 is no less than a miracle in a sport where generations are measured out in dog years. Turning 30, Tony Hawk is the grand old man of skateboarding, with a bulging sack of tricks and a proven ability to stick them like Velcro when the swag is on the table. Dude simply wakes up judges.

Hawk also owns the X Games, where he's medaled every year with incredible riding that shows what focus and professionalism is all about. His final run in the '97 Vert contest was not just the highlight of the San Diego Games, and the burliest, cleanest routine ever seen in skateboarding—it was also solid proof that extreme sports could contribute to the all-time great moments in sport, bar none.

Memo to Moms: respect the deck-obsessed child. Hawk's did, supporting him ever since he started competition skating in San Diego at age 10. Dad too. Older brother Steve, now the editor of *Surfer*, was also useful: he hooked Tony up with his first slug and probably taught him trick number one in the series of four billion to come. As for sister Pat, never mind that she once sang backup for Michael Bolton—the important thing is she quit, and now handles promotion for Tony's Birdhouse Projects, one of the biggest distributors in the industry.

Hawk is undeniably big time. He's done ads for Pepsi and Coke, and most everyone else. A stunt double in *Escape from L.A.*, he has also directed, shot and edited dozens of promo vids. In the sellout-resistant world of skateboarding, all this might suck. But thanks to his truck-hard respect for core values like aggro riding and stupid-fresh innovation, the bruddahs have no choice but to pay their props.

And now it's family. With wife Erin (an in-liner, but it's okay, really), they're sessioning with their son. "Riley is way, way too good for being four years old," says Hawk. "He is already busting ollies down little ramps. Kid's not scared of anything."

Tony Hawk, on the other hand, fears one thing: his own glittering reputation, and the expectations unleashed when he steps to the coping. "If I can't outdo what the judges think I could have done, they get bummed." Memo to Hawk: Gotta go bigger still.

BOB BURNQUIST

ONE MOMENT, YOU'RE LIVING THE DREAM, getting sent by *Thrasher* to Australia and skating 55 parks in 19 days. The next, right out of the blue, you're getting a ticket for possession of a skateboard, then having it confiscated.

On the whole, though, life's been good to Bob Burnquist, one of the friendliest and most articulate skaters on the pro circuit. Born and raised in Rio de Janeiro of an American father and a Brazilian mother, Burnquist is fluent in both English and Portuguese. Growing up idolizing pioneer Brazilian skater Lincoln Ueda, Burnquist won his first contest there at the age of 13.

Living in Daly City, CA, for the past few years, he has become a fixture of the hot San Francisco skate scene. But don't look for him to strike the pose. He isn't into the latest look or collecting all sorts of material crap. In part because of the devastation going on back in the Amazon, he's made the environment a central concern. "I wish there was something else besides wood to make skateboards out of," he says. "I don't like the deforestation idea so I ride my skateboard as much as I can so that I use it up completely." On the street or in the half-pipe, Burnquist is known for electrifying not only the crowd but fellow skaters as well: he's thrown the gauntlet in their face by building a huge repertoire of switch-stance tricks. Maybe coming from the other side of the equator helps him go both ways. "I love to skate switch as much as I can because it's like learning to skate all over again."

ANDY MACDONALD

LIVING CLEAN AND SKATING HARD, ANDY Macdonald is the poster boy for a growing "we-ain't-all-outlaws" movement in skateboarding. He's also one of the world's best ramp riders. The only man ever to beat Tony Hawk in X Games Vert competition (1996), it was only natural the pair would hook up for the inaugural Doubles competition the next year. Gold was all but inevitable.

As for life on the straight edge, Macdonald doesn't even dabble in Keystone Light. "Adrenaline is my drug," he explains. "If people pressure you to do that and don't respect how you feel, they aren't your friends."

The only thing he's hooked on is skating every day, be it street, park, drainage ditch, or whatever else you've got. For occasional variety he'll satisfy his board addiction on the snow or across the wake. And, as if he needs it, juggling helps keep his reflexes sharp.

Having competed since 1989, Macdonald has no regrets about turning pro in 1995. "In the early '90s, there was lots of attitude," he recalls, "but that's gone. It's cool to skate again." He shares that vibe with the younger generation every summer at the Woodward Skate Camp in Pennsylvania, and as the Skateboard Editor of *Digital Action*, a CD-ROM magazine. He plans to go to college "when I'm old."

Until then he'll continue to attack half-pipes like a man possessed—but by what? "Fear," says Andy Mac. "Fear keeps you in check. Fear protects you."

SKYSURFING

"CHARLIE," TO PARAPHRASE *APOCALYPSE NOW*, "DON'T SKYSURF."

Of course, G.I. Joe don't get around to it much either. But just because the number of its practioners is small, it's no reason to keep it out of the X Games. Face it: skysurfing just looks so incredibly wicked. Excitement pours off it. You probably remember the first time you ever saw some freak making like the Silver Surfer, and it was undoubtedly in a TV commercial. From its very inception, skysurfing realized how incomparably cool it was and how any product seeking public attention could do no better than to sidle up to its soaring, spinning image. Hence the Hollywood marriage of body-warping athletics with mind-roasting cinematography—a natural for the X Games, whose unprecedented broadcast coverage has put skysurfing permanently on the sporting map.

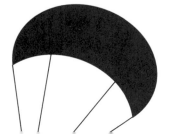

The ancient Greek myth of Icarus gives us a pretty good idea of how long human beings have been obsessed with imitating birds. Subsequent history also reveals that we haven't been terribly good about absorbing the moral of that story. It wasn't too long after the invention of airplanes, for example, that somebody decided to jump out of one.

1700s A dog attempts the first parachute jump, after being tossed from a balloon by an Englishman. Gravity 1, Dog 0. **1797** French balloonist, André-Jacques Garnerin, makes the first successful jump, albeit unscheduled. During an exhibition at a country fair, Garnerin's balloon explodes 2,000 feet above the crowd. Onlookers expect disaster, but he is able to deploy a makeshift chute and lands safely almost a mile away. Wife Genevieve and niece Elisa soon follow, the first women to jump, land and walk away. **1980** Skydivers in California experiment with "air surfing"–lying on boogie boards during freefall. **1987** Frenchman Joel Cruciani credited with first skysurfing freefall. Rigs up an ordinary surfboard with snowboard bindings for film *Hibernator*. **1989** Patrick de Gayardon invents a soft binding and cutaway system in case of emergency. **1990** Jeremy Loftis becomes the first American to skysurf. At skydiving's World Freestyle Championships in Texas, Pete McKeeman introduces the concept of a jumper and a camera flyer working together to create a video that is judged later. **1991** Mainstream America introduced to skysurfing through Reebok's "Life is Short, Play Hard" commercial. **1992** Loftis founds Surflite, a U.S. manufacturer of lightweight graphite/Kevlar skyboards. **1993** First competition takes place in Arizona, first world championships in Spain. Fittingly, a U.S./France pairing of Gus Wing and de Gayardon places first. **1994** Women's division debuts at World Championships. For Sony, Amy Baylie-Haass becomes the first woman skysurfer featured in a TV commercial. **1995** Sport gains credibility and its largest purse in the inaugural X Games, a unisex competition won by Rob Harris and Joe Jennings. Later that year, Harris dies while the pair are shooting a commercial in Canada. **1996** Jennings, now teamed with Patrick de Gayardon, scatters Harris's ashes while performing at the second X Games. **1997** Sport gets pro tour, while numbers of competitive skysurfers swells. Changes in judging encourage more variety in routines, while growing influence of freeflying techniques stimulates greater creativity.

In skysurfing, a weak early performance is hard to bounce back from. Teams made up of a skysurfer and a camera flyer make four jumps in the preliminary round, and the top five teams then make one additional jump in the final. But unlike many other X Games disciplines, cumulative average is the important number; every jump counts toward the final score. Three judges view the video of each 50-second jump and rate two components. The first is a technical mark for the difficulty and execution of the jump. The second is presentation, where artful camera work and creative team interaction come into play. This also includes a variety requirement, meaning that each jump must be substantially different from the preceding ones. Here are some of the terms you'll need to know if you're hanging out in the jump zone.

AVALANCHE A sequence where full-twisting layouts are repeated one after another. BARREL ROLL A somersault from an upright position. BIFF A parachute crash of variable severity caused when an approach and landing are misjudged. BODY ROLL A highly technical move where a skysurfer rotates parallel to the ground with arms extended. BURBLE The rough air just above a freefalling body. CHICKEN SOUP What you get when the planned move or jump routine does not go as planned. DIRT-DIVE Walking through a routine on the ground. FLAIL To be out of control during a freefall. With their additional wind-grabbing boards, skysurfers are actually in danger of dying due to violent flailing. FLOAT To rise or fall away vertically in relation to another person in freefall. FLY-BY A move in which the skysurfer tracks away from the camera flyer, turns 180 degrees and builds up horizontal speed to do a trick just as he passes the camera. FUNNEL To "steal the air" from another person, causing them both to descend faster. GALEAN Like a Sit-spin, this is grabbing the back of the board and plummeting straight down. It generates a skysurfer's highest fall rate. GYRO A transition from a Helicopter to a Sit-spin. HELICOPTER Upside-down move where the body remains vertical and the skysurfboard spins like rotors. HENHOUSE SURPRISE Grabbing the tail, arching the back and spinning in a head-down position. INVISIBLE MAN Upright spin so fast that the skysurfer seems to disappear. Can cause temporary paralysis in the distressed limbs. JACK-IN-THE-BOX Inverted camera view of a skysurfer's parachute deployment. LAY-OUT A flip from an upright to a horizontal body position. ROGAINE A rail grab move in a crouched, inverted or sit-spin layout. RING SIGHT The transparent sighting device that aims the camera flyer's lens, usually located in front of the dominant eye. SIT-SPIN Leaning all the way back, the skysurfer sits on the tail and begins to spin. SKYGOD A person of noted freefall ability, whether in fact or in his own inflated estimation. TYDY BOWL IN THE HOLE Highly difficult interactive move between partners. While the surfer goes into a Helicopter, the camera flyer flies over and then upside-down for an unusual angle. TRACKING Moving horizontally during freefall. WHUFFO A non-parachutist. From "Wha'fo' you wanna go jump outta them perfectly good planes?" Z.P. Zero-porosity, in reference to the synthetic fabrics used for canopies and the wings of a camera flyer's jumpsuit.

GOOD TO GO

Skysurfboard: $500-$750.
Camera helmet: $500.
Jumpsuit: $250. PC7 camera:
$2,500. Of course, you first
need to be certified to skydive,
which can take several weeks:
$1,500. For training at the pro
level, figure 12 jumps a day,
six days a week. At $16 a jump,
that's $1,152 per week for the
skysurfer, another $1,152 if you
want a camera flyer to record
it all for posterity. Call Daddy.

SKYSURFBOARDS ARE LIGHTWEIGHT, CUSTOM-BUILT BOARDS with a releasable binding system. Novices start out using small boards and move up to larger ones as their skills increase. Somewhere between 1/4 of an inch and 3/8 of an inch in thickness, the size is optimized as a ratio of the surface area to the skysurfer's height and weight. Skysurfboards weighing more than .6 grams per square centimeter of surface must have their own parachute recovery system.

A skysurfer wears a JUMPSUIT with "low-drag" bottoms such as Lycra sport tights to make swinging the board easier. High-drag tops create the preferred aerodynamic balance, which is similiar to that of a badminton birdie. Further drag is created by under-arm WINGLETS or mesh vents, which allow sleeves to fill with air. The higher the drag, however, the more muscle power is required to fight the wind. Camera flyers wear cotton suits with zero-porosity nylon wings from waist to hip that, when the arms are spread, quickly slow the fall.

Skysurfers use standard skydiving rigs consisting of a main CHUTE, a reserve chute and a container to hold it all. Ideally, the main chute is deployed at 2,000 to 3,000 feet. The X Games require skysurfers to use an automatic activation device or AAD, a computerized barometric sensing unit that opens the reserve parachute at a pre-set altitude if it determines that the jumper is still plummeting at high speed. Once deployed, the elliptical, wing-shaped main canopy provides the parachutist with an "inflatable glider" capable of pinpoint control and forward speeds up to 50 mph.

AIRCRAFT for the X Games is the Casa 212-200, a 30-place twin-turbine with a rear tailgate. Camera flyers have mini-cameras attached to a flat platform atop their specially designed helmets, plus a microwave transmitter that sends the signal to a land-based control truck where the action is videotaped.

TROY HARTMAN & VIC PAPPADATO Creative, smooth perfectionists.

OLIVER FURRER & CHRISTIAN SCHMID This European duo has increased their placing with every competition they enter, once beating Hartman and Pappadato. Schmid likes to rotate onto his back to film Furrer zigzagging in front of him.

TROY HARTMAN

TROY HARTMAN NEVER DREAMED of making it to the Super Bowl, but he got there anyway—albeit as a skysurfer. Perhaps you remember seeing him in two commercials that debuted during Super Bowl XXXII—in one of them, flying nonchalantly while pounding Pepsi with a goose. Proof positive that if you're looking for something that can rise above the Super-clutter, call Mr. Hartman's agent.

He can also rise above the competition. Along with camera-flying partner Vic Pappadato, Hartman copped silver, then gold, in consecutive X Games. The pair, known as diehard perfectionists, regularly pull off the unexpected. After all, it was Hartman who invented the sport's signature trick, the Henhouse Surprise. Since it was copied mercilessly by most of the other competitors, Hartman and Pappadato now keep their hyper-creative lab experiments very private until the final rounds at contest time.

Hartman began skydiving in the air force and was further inspired by the Reebok commercial featuring Patrick de Gayardon: "I basically took a piece of plywood that I found in my house," he recalls of his first naïve skysurfing effort, "threw a pair of bindings on it and jumped out of an airplane." The equipment and performance improved quickly, but skysurfing remains a risky sport. Pulling major G-forces during a spinning trick, he says, "I once burst all the blood vessels in my eyelids."

Supporting himself with jobs such as commercials and a starring role in a Wilco video, it's not surprising that Hartman sees the show business aspect of the sport taking on greater importance in future competitions. "It's like the team is a mini-production company," he says, "trying to put together a 60-second TV show. No one really knows what's next—I just fumble around until I come up with something cool."

Fortunately, he's managed to achieve that often enough to finance his competitive life. In a sport that consumes serious bank, Hartman is dumbfounded that personal sponsorship has been hard to come by. "We've tried to get backing, but the response is always negative," he reports. "Companies are interested in sponsoring the whole event but not the individual athletes. If someone would explain why, I'd love to know."

JOE JENNINGS

LIKE THE TREE THAT FALLS IN THE FOREST with nobody to hear it, a skysurfer would be nothing without his partner, the camera flyer. Joe Jennings, whose teams took X Games gold in '95 and bronze in '96, is one of the world's best.

Jennings started skydiving in the mid-'80s, and as a video hobbyist, camera-flying was a natural extension. "I used to duct-tape an audio cassette onto my left arm and scream into it while I free-fell," he remembers. "Then I saw guys with cameras mounted on their heads, so I did the same."

He hooked up with skysurfer Rob Harris, and the pair was dominant in the sport's early days. But Harris's accidental death during a jump for a soft-drink commercial in 1995 was a devastating blow to his partner. During their final jump at the next year's X Games, Jennings and new partner, French skygod Patrick de Gayardon, scattered Harris's ashes as the climactic "out" of their routine.

Now a freelance camera flyer, Jennings travels the world recording all kinds of sky-diving feats. It's a demanding job that requires both artistry and fitness. "Maintaining stability and framing is very difficult," he says, "especially when using a 35mm motion picture camera, which is really heavy. I do a lot of swimming and stretching to keep my back in alignment and my neck strong."

As for the future of skysurfing, Jennings thinks the creativity of the camera flyer will be increasingly valued by the judges, something that hasn't always been the case. "The moves are actually really difficult to master," he says, "but a lot is in the presentation, like figure skating. There has to be flair and showmanship, and the camera is a direct part of that. I mean, just documenting the jump may be fine. But if it adds dimension and feeling . . . that might be what wins the race."

DOWNHILL IN-LINE

NOT QUITE BENT ENOUGH AS IT WAS . . .

In-line racing, already a popular and growing sport, needed a little tweak if it was going to crack the X Games lineup. The solution? Send those buff bladers down a steep hill in hungry packs, and throw in a few S-curves and hay bales just for fun. This somewhat risky proposition proved to be an irresistible draw for the speed-obsessed professional in-line crew. When millions of fans—many of whom have their own in-line skates—got a close look at pros drafting, bumping and twirling off into the barnyard, it served as a visceral reminder: Maybe I'll wear those pads after all.

The idea of strapping tiny vehicles on your feet is not just old, it's ancient. Downhill in-line is the latest stop in the evolution from roller rink to roller derby.

1100 Early skates made of bone attached to leather soles are used by hunters to stalk game on ice. **1700** Skating becomes popular in lake-rich Scotland, where the first skating club is founded in Edinburgh. **MID-1700s** Belgian Joseph Merlin invents the first roller-skates, which he uses to make a radical entrance into a masquerade party while playing a violin. **1819** A French inventor patents the first documented in-line skate, consisting of two, three or four wheels in a straight line. **1863** American James Plimpton invents the modern roller-skate with two wheels side-by-side in both the front and the back. In-line wheels are relegated to history as Plimpton popularizes the new setup in roller rinks. **1884** Ball bearings introduced to a thriving roller-skating scene. **1960** A modern in-line skate is produced by the Chicago Skate Co. **1972** Raquel Welch capitalizes on the wacked-women-on-wheels thing in *Kansas City Bomber* and winds up on the cover of *Life*. **1979** Scott and Brennan Olson, two Minnesota hockey players, happen across an old in-line skate in a sporting goods store. They add urethane wheels and a rubber heel brake and find it a good summer surrogate for ice-skating. **1981** Faith in its saleability leads Scott Olson to buy Chicago Skate's in-line patent and make substantial improvements to the wheel assembly. The Rollerblade is born. **1984** Olson sells Rollerblade to Robert Naegele Jr., and the company introduces the first polyurethane boot and wheels that contain a stronger, lighter core. The number of U.S. in-line skaters reaches 20,000. **1986** Ski racers, both cross-country and downhill, start using in-line skates for cross-training. **1989** Speedskaters officially adopt in-line as a summer training activity. There are some three million in-liners worldwide. **1991** The global governing body for roller sports (FIRS) allows in-line skates in competitions for the first time. World records in the race disciplines are broken by minutes. The International In-Line Skating Association (IISA) is founded by athletes and the major in-line manufacturers. **1994** Now the fastest growing sport in the U.S., there are over 12 million in-liners worldwide. At the IISA National Championships, the length of the long-distance race doubles from 50 to 100 kilometres, described by *Inline Magazine* as "double the distance, triple the pain." **1995** X Games delivers in-line to millions of homes around the world with the first exclusively downhill race, won by Derek Downing. **1996** With Downing injured, Dante Muse skates to victory in the second X Games. Women's division debuts. Despite being "scared to death," Gypsy Tidwell skates away in the final. **1997** Controversy dogs the sport as a new sanctioning organization called USA Inline Racing challenges the dominance of the U.S. Amateur Confederation of Roller Skating. At the X Games, intentionally slow starts and drafting figure prominently in the event's evolving strategy. Tidwell and Downing win repeat golds. With Nike and Fila now manufacturing skate boots, the sport is marked for continued rapid growth.

X GAMES DOWNHILL COMPETITION begins with each racer making two solo runs, from which the best time is taken and the field is seeded accordingly. After that, racers go off in brackets of four, with the top two finishers advancing to the next round. Higher seeds are given better lanes, as judged by race organizers. The races are supervised by a dozen officials, who watch for such things as cursing, unsportsmanlike conduct or dissing a fellow competitor. Penalties range from whole-second deductions (up to five) to complete disqualification for severe violations.

Once a race starts, the officials focus on course infractions. The rules of downhill in-line racing are very similar to those of bicycle racing: there must be no blocking or cutting off another competitor. Still, a racer's arms are swinging freely, so officials are on the lookout for a grab or a push in the heat of battle. Sometimes you'll see a racer drafting behind another and since that causes the follower to gain speed on the one fighting the wind, a hand placed in the small of the lead skater's back helps them both go faster, and is acceptable. The timing and placement is monitored electronically, but officials also verify the winner by eye. A racer isn't through until the lead skate, with wheels on the ground, crosses the electric eye at the finish line.

The men's races at San Diego marked the first time that X Game competitors elected to start in a slow, strategic fashion. Like bicycle pursuit racing, skaters play cat-and-mouse for the first quarter of the race until someone bursts from the pack and triggers an all-out sprint. Along with drafting and slingshotting, it's part of the rapid evolution that makes downhill one of the most dynamic events at the X Games.

ABEC The degree of precision of a wheel bearing. The higher the number, the smoother the wheel. **BLACK ICE** A very smooth, recently paved street. **CIRCUIT RACE** A multi-lap event on a course usually two miles or more in length that includes some climbing. **CRITERIUM** A multi-lap event on a flat course, usually of a mile or less in length. **DOMESTIQUE** The French word for servant, it applies to team racing in which one racer is designated the top dog and the others must do everything in their power to help that skater win, including throw themselves down in front of the pack. **DOWN START** Type of start where the racer looks like a track runner in the block. The back leg is down and the hands are on the ground. **DRAFTING** Skating close behind another skater, in the so-called slipstream. The lead skater expends up to 30 percent more energy than the drafting skater. Drafting permits the follower to store up energy in order to slingshot past and take the lead. **FLYER** A single skater who charges ahead of a large pack of skaters. **HOOK** To move over, either intentionally or by accident, and impede a skater who is trying to pass. Also, *block*. **ICE START** Feet are placed with toes apart in a "duck walk" position. Some skaters start with their bodies angled up to 90 degrees to the starting line. **JUMP** A sudden acceleration, often at the start of a sprint. **KICK** The final burst of speed in a sprint. **LATE PASS** A pass made by sneaking inside another skater just before a turn pylon. **LEAD-OUT** Leading a teammate, breaking the wind resistance and allowing him or her to sprint ahead to the finish. **POWER PASS** A pass made on a straightaway, using raw leg power to overtake. **ROAD RASH** Scrapes incurred from falling on cement or pavement. **T-STOP** The main method of stopping, in which the wheels of the trailing skate are dragged perpendicular to arrest momentum.

As the leading downhill race of its kind, the X Games has its own strategies and vocabulary. But if you hang around the speed-skating scene, you're liable to hear many of these terms.

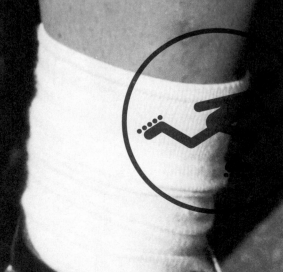

GOOD TO GO
Verducci Pro-Fit racing
boot, customized for
Julie Brandt: $1,000. Standard
racing boots: $500-$600.
Frame: $250 (includes axle kit).
Bearings: $75 for a pack of 20.
Wheels: $90 for a set of 10.
Helmet: $100. Pads: $40 -$100.

RACING SKATES HAVE THE SAME basic components as aggressive skates, but there are differences. The BOOT is lighter and better ventilated, using materials like fiberglass or Kevlar. Some more expensive models are vacuum-fit around a plaster cast of the skater's foot. Down-hill skates have a FRAME or CHASSIS that is thicker and more rigid, since any flexing in the frame dissipates the energy of a skater's push.

The big difference between recreational skates and pro in-line speedskates is the number of WHEELS. Rec skates usually have four wheels; speedskates have five and in some cases six, plus a longer wheelbase. Racers like their wheels larger (around 80 mm) and softer, to absorb shock from the uneven road. They also prefer non-ABEC-rated Swiss BEARINGS, the best money can buy.

Lycra rules as the LOW-DRAG CLOTHING of choice. And because down-hill involves dangers that racers don't normally encounter in flatland and long-distance events, a full kit of WRIST, KNEE and ELBOW PADS complements an aerodynamic bicycle HELMET.

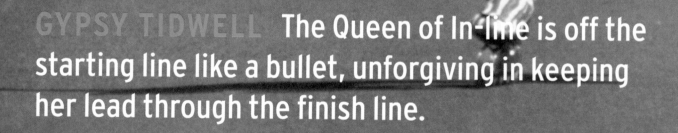

GYPSY TIDWELL The Queen of In-line is off the starting line like a bullet, unforgiving in keeping her lead through the finish line.

JULIE BRANDT Fast, fast, fast, but not as fast as Tidwell when it counts. Yet.

JESSICA APGAR It's all in the Apgar family: Mom skates Masters, sisters slow down and go for artistry while Jessica muscled past the rest of the field in her first X Games to grab the bronze in '97.

DEREK DOWNING The competitive speedster is ready to blow by anyone in his way, wheels hissing through the tight corners. Has captured numerous national and world titles in indoor in-line racing.

TONY MUSE World speed champ at 17, the most decorated athlete in in-line history is great at velocity, a tad tentative on descents and in corners.

DANTE MUSE While the younger Muse backs off in the clutch, older bro Dante charges to the finish line. Mellow in street shoes, this Muse is an inferno on skates.

G

GIVE JULIE BRANDT CREDIT FOR KEEPING HER GOALS both practical and clearly in focus. Going into her second X Games, she told reporters, "I want to place in the top four without killing myself." An understandable hope considering that the previous year she'd been the fastest X Games qualifier but crashed in the final, albeit without injury. Still, she overcame the residual fear and achieved her goal the next time out—in 1997 she wound up in second place, trailing Gypsy Tidwell by little more than a wheel's diameter.

Jules, as she's known on the professional in-line racing circuit, started competing on quads back in 1989, at the tender age of 10. Since then she's proved herself to be a contender in every event from 500 meters to 100-kilometer ultra-distance marathons. With versatility like that, it's no wonder she also rages in downhill. "The X Games are fun," she says. "Because it's the only downhill event we skate, you don't find the normal pressure. It's still competitive, but because a hill is added, it's more of a fun thing." Living in Huntington Beach, CA, Brandt is fortunate to be able to train year-round. "I skate open road, which means touring 10 miles out and back, and closed circuit, doing laps indoors on a 100-meter track," she says. "I also do a lot of cross-training like cycling." She is both sponsored by and works for Verducci, a manufacturer of in-line boots and frames owned by her husband. Eventually, however, she plans to attend college, "so I can play more of an important role within the business." Meanwhile, she'll keep on racing—for the cash, if nothing else. "This year," she says with a big smile, "if you went down the hill, you basically got 200 bucks. Hey, that's a big-money race for speed skaters!"

JULIE BRANDT

GYPSY TIDWELL

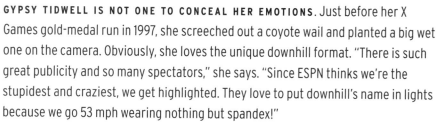

GYPSY TIDWELL IS NOT ONE TO CONCEAL HER EMOTIONS. Just before her X Games gold-medal run in 1997, she screeched out a coyote wail and planted a big wet one on the camera. Obviously, she loves the unique downhill format. "There is such great publicity and so many spectators," she says. "Since ESPN thinks we're the stupidest and craziest, we get highlighted. They love to put downhill's name in lights because we go 53 mph wearing nothing but spandex!"

The 23-year-old from Waco, TX, practically grew up in a roller rink and began competing at the age of two. Coached for a long time by her father (now coach of the French World Team), she is a talented sprinter who in 1994 became the world's fastest female in-liner. Having undergone her share of knocks as a young pup breaking into adult ranks, Tidwell was ready for the rough-and-tumble of downhill.

"It's difficult to get friendship and camaraderie together all the time," she says. "Everybody is a back-stabber once in their life . . . in skating, maybe five or six times."

These days, though, Tidwell keeps the attitude under control. As a married woman and the manager of a skating rink, she understands limits. "I would love to have something pierced or a tattoo," she says, looking around at her X Games contemporaries, "but I have to be professional in my job, to be respected by the parents of the kids I coach. I consider myself a role model."

DEREK DOWNING

WITH ICE SPEEDSKATING A LONGTIME WINTER OLYMPIC SPORT, a certain faction of the in-line world is lobbying to get wheeled speedskaters in there as well. But don't expect Derek Downing to get too excited about it. "As long as there are the X Games," he says, "the Olympics don't matter." Needless to say, the X Games have been good to both Downing and his sport. As champion in 1995's inaugural event, he's been first in line to benefit from the boom in public awareness that it helped foster. "It's the best thing that ever happened to our sport," he says. "No one knew what it was before that—the X Games just put us on the map."

Downing had indeed toiled away for some time without the world taking notice. The sport is in his blood—he is a fourth-generation skater whose parents had him on blades before he could walk. And despite his aggressive speed and highly competitive nature, he's gained a reputation for being a genuinely nice guy. "If everyone hates you," he says, "you're in for a world of hurt."

Following a year's absence after breaking his collarbone in five places, Downing returned to the X Games in 1997 and reclaimed the top of the podium. This latest gold had him contemplating retirement and coaching younger athletes, but that soon passed. "I think I'm going to ride it out for the next couple of years," he says, adding that even when he decides to hang them up, "I'll probably still do the downhill at the X Games."

AGGRESSIVE IN-LINE

KILL . . . OR BE KILLER.

In the violent version of the future portrayed in the film *Rollerball*, professional roller-skating was more than just a blood sport, it was a life-or-death proposition. Now that 1975's future has arrived, we know that director Norman Jewison was close, if not exactly clairvoyant. Sure, there would still be roller and there would still be balls. But as for the gladiatorial pain, these days it's all self-inflicted, in a restless struggle to perform stunts that defy the laws of both physics and good sense. At the end of the century, the only thing that gets murdered by aggressive in-line skaters is that little voice inside everyone that says, Slow down . . . take it easy . . . not so high.

Aggressive in-lining was, in the beginning, ignored by the racing community and actively loathed by the skateboarders whose playgrounds it was invading.

1975 James Caan defines full-out aggro in *Rollerball*. **1981** People like A.J. Jackson, Pat Parnell, Doug Boyce and Chris Morris start using in-lines on the same types of Street and Vert terrain as skateboarders. Tricks borrowed from skateboarding include Method Airs and inverts. The industry, however, ignores the phenomenon. **1988** Rollerblade introduces the Lighting TRS, the first skate with a nylon-reinforced frame. The innovation allows skaters to experience the thrill of grinding; Chris Edwards is said to be the first in-liner to scrape a handrail for an entire flight of stairs. **1989** Rollerblade introduces the Tarmac and begins to organize contests. Small manufacturers of aggressive in-line equipment begin to appear. *Skater* begins publishing. **1990** As the number of in-liners in the U.S. reaches one million, a second wave of aggressive skaters comes on the scene. *In-line* begins publishing. **1991** A.J. Jackson meets a young Arlo Eisenberg at a demo and tells him to go west. Aggressive tricks become more diversified and more difficult. **1993** *Daily Bread* and *Box* start publishing. The first aggressive video is released. **1994** The first National In-line Skater Series (NISS) takes place. **1995** Aggressive Skater's Association is formed, and the sport's debut in the X Games lends it long-sought legitimacy—and a glimpse of the sport's international future. Australian Matt Salerno wins the gold in Street, even though it is the 16-year-old's first big competition. **1996** Aggressive skating teams up with skateboarding and bicycle stunt for a multi-sport tour of America that culminates in a wild, choreographed exhibition at the closing ceremonies of the Olympics. At the X Games, Fabiola de Silva takes the first of two consecutive Vert golds. **1997** The guard changes: Aaron Feinberg wins X Games gold in Street on his 16th birthday. But he's ancient compared to 12-year-old Women's Vert bronze medalist, Ayumi Kawasaki, the youngest X athlete ever.

IN YOUR TYPICAL HOME-GROWN AGGRESSIVE session at the local park, you skate a bit, then you hang a bit, watching the others go off. The X Games may feel similar, but the one big difference is the limited time frame. You might be the best skater, but if you don't nail your tricks when the spotlight's on, there's no such thing as making it up to the bros later on with an extra-sick move.

The time limit is 50 seconds in Vert and 65 in Street. In both disciplines the preliminary round consists of two runs, from which the average score yields the top 10 men (in a field of 24), and the top four of eight women. Seven judges render their opinions in four components: Style, Difficulty, Consistency and Line. Each is worth 25 points, for a possible total of 100.

The final round consists of three runs, in the reverse order of the preliminary round leaderboard. The lowest of the three scores is thrown out, and whoever has the highest average of the other two is declared the winner. For the final round only, in the event of a tie for first place, a run-off occurs with the highest score taking the gold.

Aggressive in-line is still a young sport, one that's evolving in different environments (including off-road) around the world. At the '97 X Games, there were 11 countries represented, with an age range from 12 to 26. Consequently you'll continue to see such a surprising variety of spins, grabs and grinds that sometimes the judges don't even know what they like best until they see it at the X Games.

STYLE How much soul is being put on the table. In other words, whether the skater most resembles a cherry El Dorado or a cancerous Yugo.

DIFFICULTY The tricks' degree of technicality, combined with how big the skater busts 'em.

CONSISTENCY How sticky the landings are, and how fresh the skating is at the end of the run compared to the beginning.

LINE A factor of how innovatively the tricks are linked together. In Street, judges look for the skater's creative use of maximum terrain.

BIO GRAB Grabbing the outside of the skate with the hand on the same side. BRAINLESS A Backflip with a 540-degree turn. BUDGET VARIATION A variation in which the position of one skate is changed during the trick. CAMEL A toe-tap upon re-entry into the pipe. CROSSED A grab with the hand opposite the skate. CROSSED UP Performing a trick with legs crossed. FARSIDE When a trick is performed on the outside or far edge of the ramp. FAST SLIDE A one-skate grind. HAND PLANT One hand grabs the skate while doing a one-handed handstand on the ramp or obstacle. MILLER FLIP A backflip with a 360-degree turn. MISTY FLIP A front somersault with a 540 spin, first popularized by Ryan Jacklone. MUTE A crossed-grab air. NATURAL The position in which the skater feels most comfortable performing a trick, with either the right or left skate forward. REWIND A spin performed coming off a grind or stall. SOUL GRIND Keeping the leading skate parallel to the rail and the rear skate perpendicular. STALE Grabbing the wheels during a trick. STALL Landing on a lip and pausing before re-entry. VARIATION Changing from one type of grind or grab to another while doing a long trick like a rail grind. WALLRIDE Riding on a wall that has no transition.

25

25

25

25

100

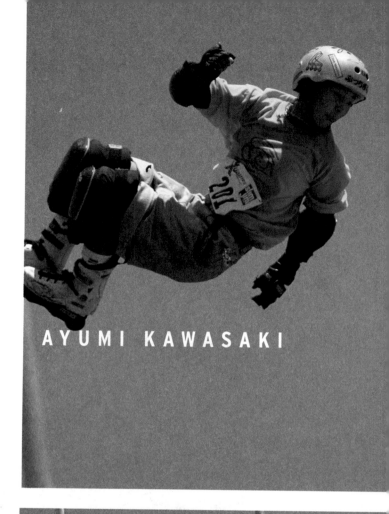

AYUMI KAWASAKI

IN SPORTS LIKE THESE, nobody is safe from the invasion of the unbelievably young and talented. But 12 years old? That's what Ayumi Kawasaki was when she became the youngest X Games competitor in history en route to a third-place finish in Vert. Part of the burgeoning Japanese force in in-line, Kawasaki amazed her elders by busting adult-sized grabs and slides, plus hard tricks like 720 McTwists. "That's the beauty of being 12," marveled fellow in-liner Distel Pipe, who watched in disbelief as Kawasaki ripped up the ramp, all the while displaying an air of happy relaxation. "You don't think about it, you just do it. The problem with getting old is that you start thinking too much."

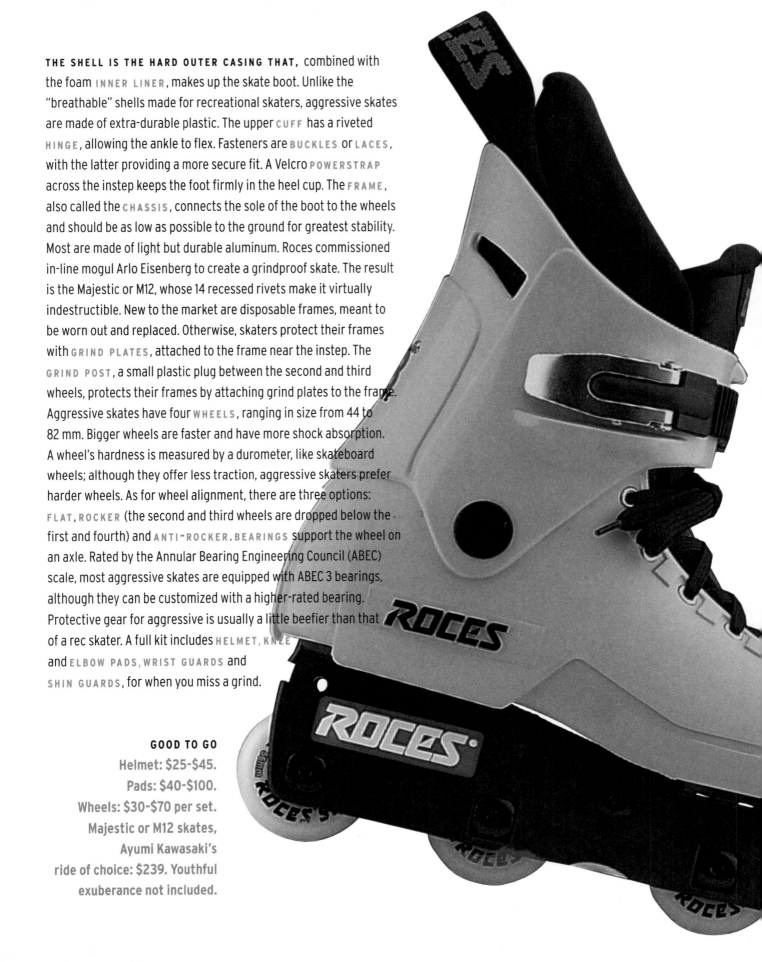

THE SHELL IS THE HARD OUTER CASING THAT, combined with the foam INNER LINER, makes up the skate boot. Unlike the "breathable" shells made for recreational skaters, aggressive skates are made of extra-durable plastic. The upper CUFF has a riveted HINGE, allowing the ankle to flex. Fasteners are BUCKLES or LACES, with the latter providing a more secure fit. A Velcro POWERSTRAP across the instep keeps the foot firmly in the heel cup. The FRAME, also called the CHASSIS, connects the sole of the boot to the wheels and should be as low as possible to the ground for greatest stability. Most are made of light but durable aluminum. Roces commissioned in-line mogul Arlo Eisenberg to create a grindproof skate. The result is the Majestic or M12, whose 14 recessed rivets make it virtually indestructible. New to the market are disposable frames, meant to be worn out and replaced. Otherwise, skaters protect their frames with GRIND PLATES, attached to the frame near the instep. The GRIND POST, a small plastic plug between the second and third wheels, protects their frames by attaching grind plates to the frame. Aggressive skates have four WHEELS, ranging in size from 44 to 82 mm. Bigger wheels are faster and have more shock absorption. A wheel's hardness is measured by a durometer, like skateboard wheels; although they offer less traction, aggressive skaters prefer harder wheels. As for wheel alignment, there are three options: FLAT, ROCKER (the second and third wheels are dropped below the first and fourth) and ANTI-ROCKER. BEARINGS support the wheel on an axle. Rated by the Annular Bearing Engineering Council (ABEC) scale, most aggressive skates are equipped with ABEC 3 bearings, although they can be customized with a higher-rated bearing. Protective gear for aggressive is usually a little beefier than that of a rec skater. A full kit includes HELMET, KNEE and ELBOW PADS, WRIST GUARDS and SHIN GUARDS, for when you miss a grind.

GOOD TO GO
Helmet: $25-$45.
Pads: $40-$100.
Wheels: $30-$70 per set.
Majestic or M12 skates,
Ayumi Kawasaki's
ride of choice: $239. Youthful
exuberance not included.

CHRIS EDWARDS (VERT & STREET) Fluid, fast and smooth, he's one of the Godfathers of aggressive in-line, yet can still take the new kids to school on the street.

ARLO EISENBERG (VERT & STREET) Innovative, outspoken, artistic, Eisenberg is now bringing up the next wave at Senate, including Randy "Roadhouse" Spizer.

TIM WARD (VERT & STREET) The Natural. An avid 24/7 skater, this Australian is breaking international barriers.

AARON FEINBERG (STREET) A Street powerhouse despite his small frame. His revolutionary vision on the course, flight rotations and flips with perfect landings to transition provide a glimpse of things to come in in-line.

FABIOLA DE SILVA (VERT) In tune with the life, adaptive to the extreme, insane about big air, she's the leader of the international pack.

AYUMI KAWASAKI (VERT) Relaxed, happy and determined, this 12-year-old is the future of women's aggro in-line.

SAYAKA YABE (STREET) Part of the Japanese stronghold starting to sweep the industry and contest scene. Yabe pulls out effortless grinds, airs and carves, and is one of the few women to utilize the handrail in competition.

CHRIS EDWARDS

AT 24, CHRIS EDWARDS IS A WILY VETERAN of aggressive in-line, lucky enough to have learned from the age of 12 from some big-name older skaters. He was a quick study. By 1987, he started a relationship with Rollerblade that eventually led to his own signature model of skate. Known for his speed, high air and creative use of terrain, Edwards has medaled in three consecutive X Games.

His long tenure at the top of the sport has given Edwards considerable perspective. "Before 1994," he recalls, "it was basically grassroots. We did demos in front of stores with 20 people watching. Now there are local and regional events with 200 to 300 kids who can outskate us old-school guys." Some of the changes have affected the heart and soul of the sport, says Edwards, and there have been some setbacks. "I don't see any more money for us, but I'm confident and determined that it will get better. I mean, the sport is really still too new and young. We're not quite legitimate yet."

As for his skating, Edwards approaches it very much like a veteran: "I prepare more mentally than physically. That's the number one thing for me. Skating is more like a lifestyle, an expression of my inner being. I can go a month without skating, but if I am mentally prepared, it'll flow."

Edwards's gear company, Birth Clothing, has recently started to take off. And now he has another dream: buying an RV and traveling the U.S. promoting aggressive skating. "I want to set up mini-ramps in front of stores and tie in the industry. I want to make sure that kids can still do this 10 years from now, and that people will strive for a sense of friendship, integrity and harmony." Or, to put it another way, he wants to "tear down the baseball diamonds and build skateparks."

He just might succeed. Says the hardcore old-schooler who has yet to break a bone: "God has seven angels around me."

AARON FEINBERG

ARLO EISENBERG

AT THE AGE OF 24, YOU DON'T NECESSARILY EXPECT TO PASS the torch to a new generation. But maybe that comes with the territory in the light-speed evolution of aggressive in-line. Whatever the case, Arlo Eisenberg was the first to congratulate Aaron Feinberg for his X Games Street victory, welcoming the youngster into what promises to be a long tenure in the sport's elite ranks.

The date was June 27, 1997, notable because it was Feinberg's 16th birthday. With the power and precision of a seasoned pro, the pint-sized charger nailed flips, rotations and difficult technical grinds. As he left the course after his final run, Feinberg was jubilantly spun around by Eisenberg and lifted to the shoulders of Chris Edwards. Birthdays simply don't get much better than that.

As for Eisenberg, who placed fifth that day, it was nothing to be bummed about. "I'm starting to come to terms with my performance," says the skater who has emblematized aggressive in-line to the outside world. "What's important to me is that I enjoy it. Every time I compete I want to win, but at this point in my career, it's not live or die." In fact, Eisenberg has already achieved most of his in-line goals, including a founding partnership in the Senate skate company and a family-owned skatepark back in Dallas.

All that plus getting your butt kicked by some punk not even old enough to drive? It's all part of the sport's maturation, says the not-so-reluctant mentor. One thing's for sure: "I don't envy the judges. It's hard to pick the best—the difference between first and 10th place can be so minor. If it's any indication of where the sport is going, then watch out."

IT'S OFFICIAL: THE SPIRIT OF THE X GAMES HAS ROCKED THE WORLD. At the '97 edition, international competitors represented 23 countries and about one-third of the 450 athletes. And there's no better evidence of the power from overseas than women's aggressive in-line.

Meet Brazilian Fabiola de Silva and Sayaka Yabe of Japan. Although they are worlds apart in geography and culture, each killed it in her respective Vert and Street finals. It didn't matter what mother tongue their fellow competitors used—being left speechless is the same in any language. Take a glimpse at their home lives, and you'll see some elements that look familiar and others that might seem strange.

De Silva was a repeat winner at the '97 X Games, having dominated Vert since her first North American competition in 1996. A former kickboxer, she lives in Sao Paolo, one of the world's biggest metropolises, where she likes to listen to groups such as Deep Forest and 311. Her favorite food is a black bean dish called *feijoada*.

Yabe, meanwhile, works in Tokyo as a machine operator in a pharmaceutical firm. The four-foot-11-inch street dynamo likes to session at a spot called Amazing Skate Park and fuel up afterwards on burgers. Although she can rattle off the names of hundreds of aggressive tricks, she speaks little English. And as for the law-enforcement climate for Japanese street skaters, Yabe reports that she has performed handrail grinds and had policemen come up and say, Good luck!

Now if only we could import *that*.

FABIOLA DE SILVA

SAYAKA YABE

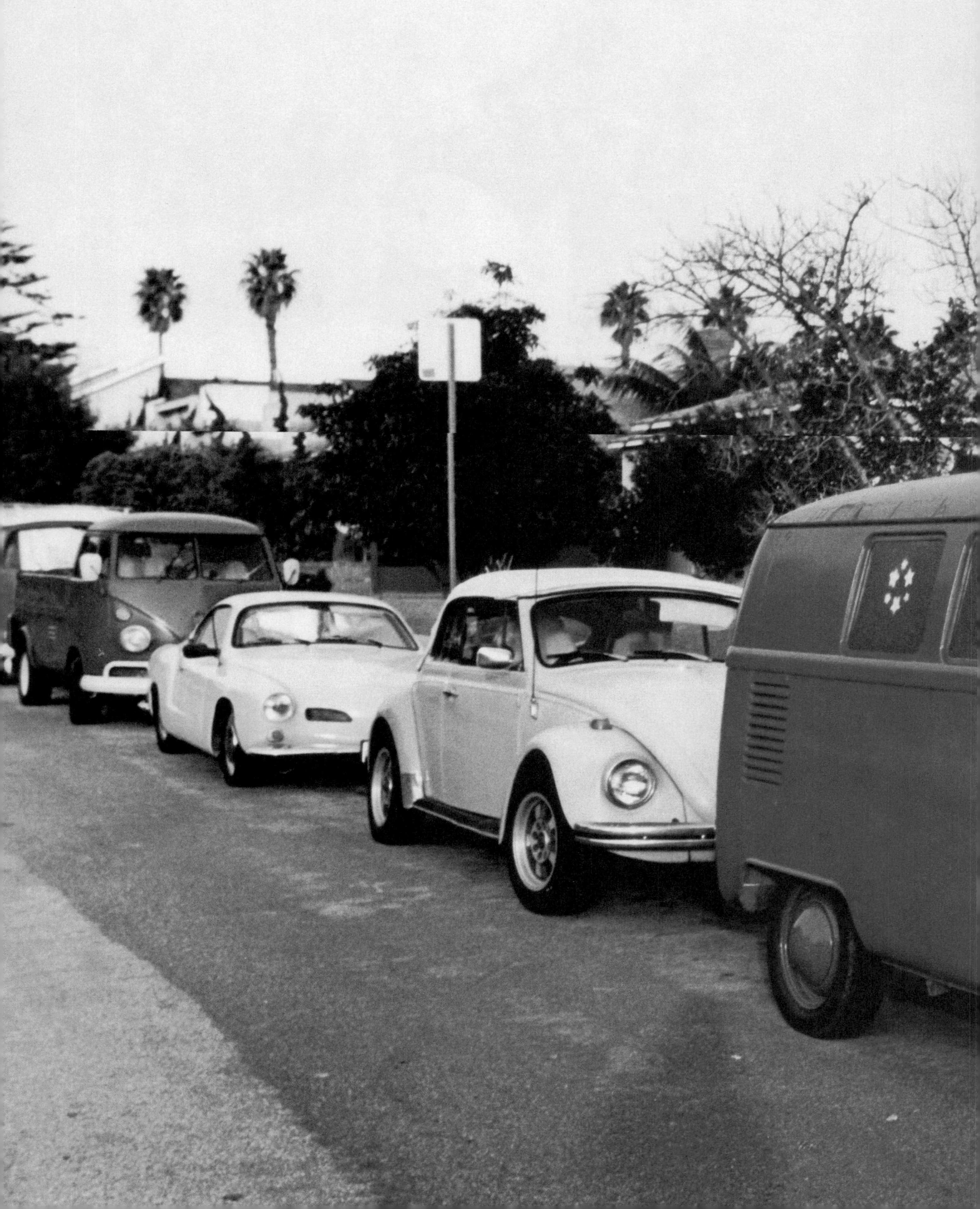

STREET LUGE

STREET LUGERS ARE PINCHING THEMSELVES.

Can this be real? It seems like just seconds ago they were skulking around freshly paved backroads, middle of the night, scanning the horizon for cops as they put the final tweaks on their jury-rigged skateboards and screwed up their courage for a heart-stopping plunge into the asphalt abyss. Talk about underground—even BASE-jumpers used to enjoy more visibility than street luge pilots. But things changed, and fast. It seems that kids around the world made the parallel discovery that true skateboard speed could only be generated by going booty-first. Pretty soon there were sanctioned events featuring custom-built sleds, timing to the hundredth second, brand-new leathers with real sponsor logos, even hay bales. And it took place in the daytime! Legally! Unreal, man.

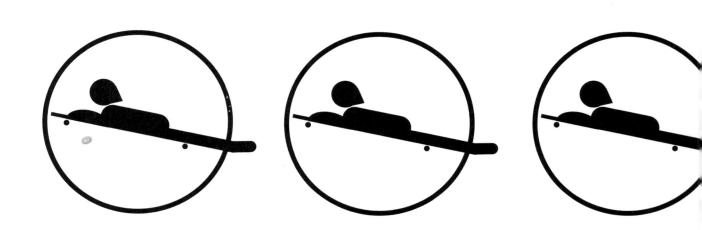

The origins of street luge are difficult to trace. It seems to have undergone what Charles Darwin would have called "parallel evolution." California lugers claim to have invented it; so does a crew from Washington State. South Americans have been doing it for years on twisting highways in the Andes. But the fact is, kids have been risking their necks in gravity vehicles since long before even soapbox derbies. Modern street luge, however, is directly related to skateboarding, because wherever people have skateboarded, they have also experimented with the faster and much less scary technique of sitting on the deck.

1970s During the second coming of the skateboard, California riders start sitting on their decks and racing one another. They call it "butt-boarding." In Washington State, Lee Dansie and friends conduct their own speed experiments. 1978 Racers build head-first, fiberglass-enclosed vehicles and compete on Signal Hill in California. About a third of them crash, injuring spectators and, it is rumored, killing one pilot. 1980 Lugers create the "Signal Hill Rules," forbidding enclosed cockpits, truck widths greater than a foot and wheels in excess of five inches. The first organized luge race takes place on the legendary Glendora Mountain Road. Luger Darren Lott is pictured on the cover of *SkateBoarder;* inside, there's another photo of him receiving a ticket. Meanwhile, L.A. enacts an ordinance forbidding any skateboard on a hill steeper than a three percent grade and from going faster than 10 mph. 1984 Bob Pereyra is featured in a television program that exposes and legitimizes street luge for the first time. He tinkers with custom designs; Lee Dansie works on a more sledlike luge. 1988 The Jamaican bobsled team brings Jah Power to the Winter Olympics, later immortalized in the John Candy flick *Cool Runnings.* 1990 Seeking to shake the sport's outlaw image, Pereyra founds RAIL (Road Racers Association for International Luge). 1992 The first of the squabbling between rival sanctioning bodies that dogs the sport: Roger Hickey forms FIGR (Federation of International Gravity Racing). 1993 RAIL puts the sport in front of 100,000 motorsport fans at Laguna Seca Raceway in Monterey, CA. 1994 Roger Hickey's integrity is called into question when, at the start of the season, he already has "1994 World Champion" sewn on his leathers. 1995 Street luge debuts at the X Games, its biggest exposure to date. 1996 The FIGR, now called Extreme Downhill International, is bought by X Games Mass Luge champion Biker Sherlock. 1997 Street luge becomes one of the most popular events at the X Games. Many of the competitors had been inspired by watching the event on TV two years earlier. Yet another organization, the International Gravity Sports Association, is founded by Marcus Rietema, "to bring everyone together."

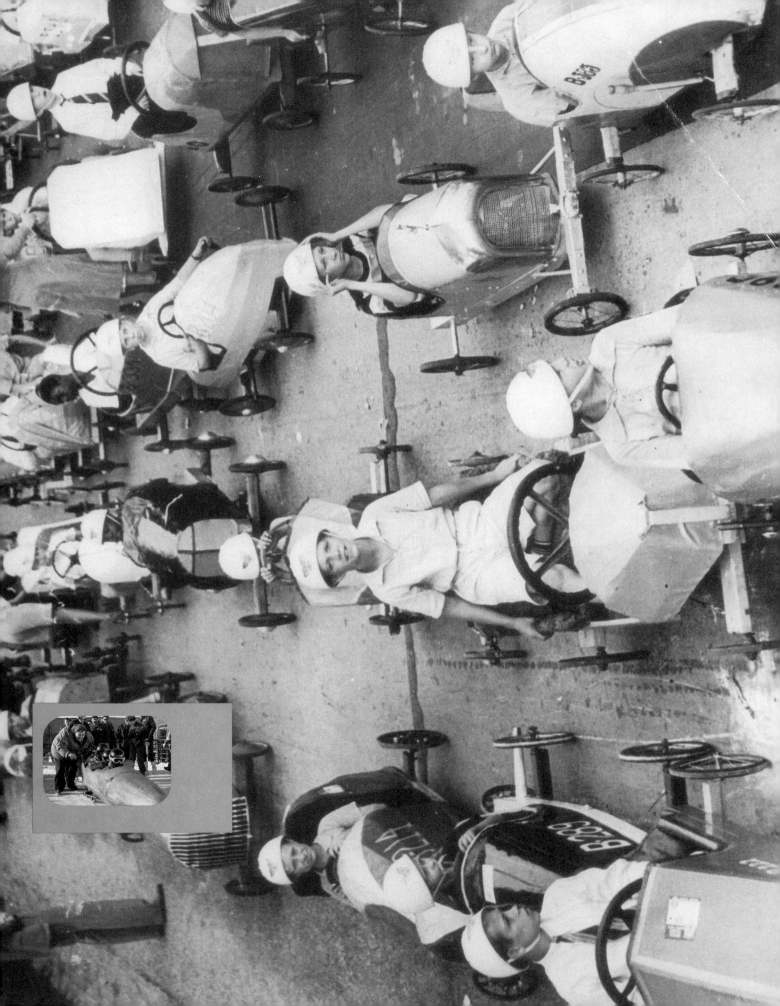

FAR FROM THE AD HOC REGULATION OF ITS UNDERGROUND BEGINNINGS, street luge at the X Games runs like a well-oiled machine. The race officials consist of one Starter, two Paddle Line/Lane Judges, one Blend Line Judge, five Course Marshals and a Chief Steward. Competition begins with each pilot from the field of 50 making two solo, timed runs. The fastest of the two is taken to compile qualifying rankings. The top 32 become eligible for Dual and Mass, while Super Mass can accommodate a field of 48.

Following qualification, time is no longer a factor. What matters is finish placement in single-elimination, bracketed competition. In Dual, the winner goes on while the loser goes home. In Mass, which features four racers, the top two advance. And in Super Mass, three of six move on to the next race.

The course has a start house with six lanes. Pushing with the hands is allowed only in the Paddle Zone. (An exception is made in the event of re-entering the race after a crash.) After that, there is a stretch called the Glide Zone where racers must remain in their lanes. Only upon passing the Blend Line may they start jockeying for position. Racers face disqualification for violations of these rules or for making a false start. If the Course Marshals notice any improper blocking or bumping, they have the power to disqualify the offending racer. Otherwise, a pilot himself may protest a perceived violation, which the Chief Steward must rule upon before the next race may start.

From the athlete's perspective, raw speed depends on equipment quality and the ability to make one's body as aerodynamic as possible. As for strategy, the major decision is whether to paddle out fast and first, or hang back to take advantage of drafting. If the leader can prevent a slingshot pass in the race's final stages, the early-lead strategy pays off. Meanwhile, in traffic, the idea is to "outbrake" opponents—in other words, brake just after they do when entering a corner. There are two ways to slow down a street luge: by dragging one's feet or by sitting more upright to increase wind resistance. Most riders choose a combination of the two.

Racers' leathers aren't the only colorful feature of the sport. With a pedigree derived equally from skateboarding and stock car racing, it's hardly surprising that a healthy crop of jargon has grown up around street luge.

AMPED Filled with the adrenaline rush that comes from luge racing. **APEX** The part of a corner where the luge is nearest to the inside of the corner. **BACON** Very rough and hazardous road surface conditions. **BANANA** A luger who wipes out often. **BLOWN GERMAN** What Stefan Wagner and his countrymen call their radical lean into the corners, which they claim keeps stability on all four wheels. **DROP A HILL** To run a luge course. **DRAFT** As in motorsports, this occurs when a pilot tucks in behind another racer, sheltering from the full force of the headwind and gathering speed for a bid to slingshot past. To get the full benefit of draft, the rear pilot must be no further than one sled-length behind. **EDI (EXTREME DOWNHILL INTERNATIONAL)** The luge governing body formerly know as FIGR (Federation of International Gravity Racing), founded by luging great Roger Hickey. Ownership passed from Hickey to Perry Fisser in 1996, then to Biker Sherlock later that year. EDI races are weekend-long events that include stand-up skateboarding, luge racing and Gravity Formula One racing. The top five riders in the EDI standings get a guaranteed spot in the X Games. **FLAME** When wheels actually catch fire as a result of the friction associated with high speeds. See also *puke*. **FLESH WING** To extend an arm for balance during a run. **FLOWING WATER** The ultimate luge riding style in which the pilot befriends gravity by perfectly emulating the path of water running down a mountain road. **HYSTERIA** Uncontrolled speed wobbles. **IGSA (INTERNATIONAL GRAVITY SPORTS ASSOCIATION)** Another sanctioning body whose competitions produce qualifiers for the X Games, this one is run by Marcus Rietema. He hopes to open the rules to more types of luge construction, thereby enabling more people to compete and bringing more riders together. **LEATHERS** The leather suits worn by luge pilots to minimize abrasions (or *road rash*) in the event of a crash. Similar to those used by motorcycle road racers. **PADDLE APRON** The designated area at the start in which racers propel themselves by pushing with their hands. **PUKE A WHEEL** To blow up or liquefy a wheel due to the extreme heat of traveling at high speeds. Also *melt, spew*. **RAIL (ROAD RACERS ASSOCIATION FOR INTERNATIONAL LUGE)** Another governing body, founded by Bob Pereyra in the 1980s. The top five racers in the RAIL standings automatically qualify for the X Games. **SCRAMBLED EGGS** Road conditions that are bad but usable. **SCREAMING MIMIS** High-speed sound and vibrations of the unhealthy kind. **SCRUB A WHEEL** To remove manufacturing residue and other gunk from a new wheel by using it in a short warm-up session. **SLED** Most common name for luge board. Also *rail*. **STOPPIES** The crowd-pleasing method for stopping the luge in a hurry: lifting the front of the board while standing up quickly. Also called *quickstop*. **WAD** To crash into a large group. **WAIL** To go extremely fast. **WOBBS** Speed wobbles, in which the rear suspension is improperly adjusted, causing it to veer left and right (the resulting steering vibration may cause a violent rollover). Usually indicate a malfunction and require the pilot to slow down at once.

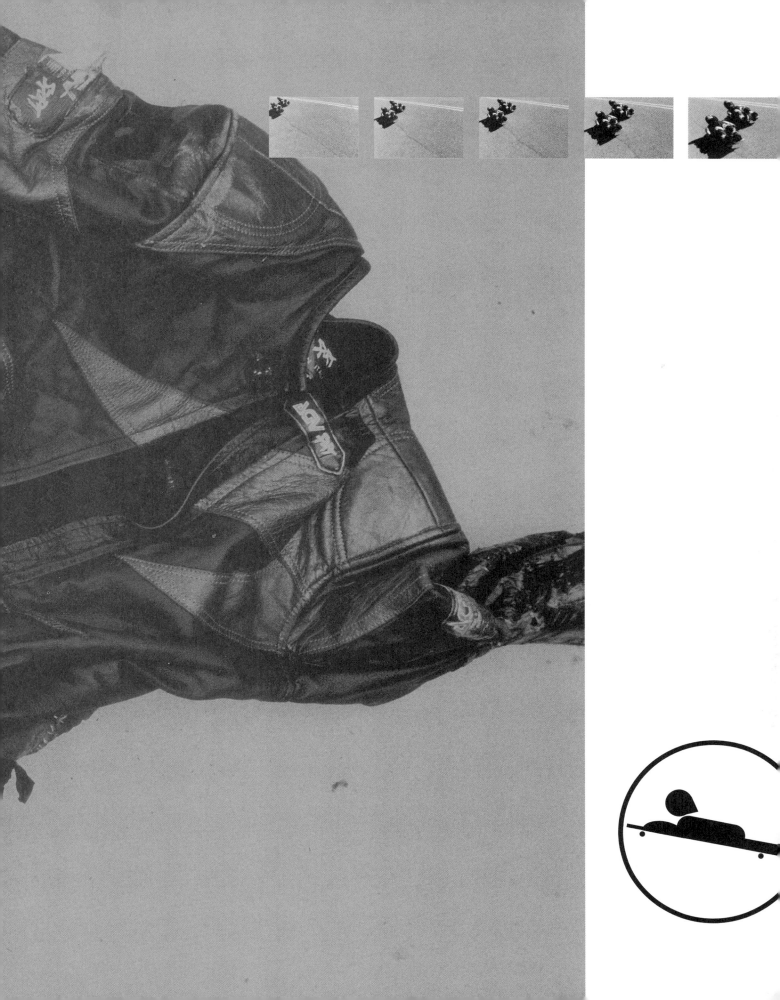

BIKER SHERLOCK'S DREGS PRO MODEL street luge, designed by aerospace engineer Jarret "Dr. Gofast" Ewanek, is the first board built using computer-aided design (CAD) throughout. It features an exclusive TORSION BAR with adjustable torsional and longitudinal flex, which allows precise chassis tuning for different courses. (It's like having a pair of skis that could be either flexible slalom skis or stiff grand slalom skis.) Biker's luge also has easily adjustable FOOT PEGS. Because foot peg placement differs according to the pilot's height, this feature is helpful if you're sharing a luge or teaching another rider. Dr. Gofast also added an advanced DIFFUSER behind the seat, which dissipates turbulence, reduces drag and throws a minimum draft. **Price: $1,800**

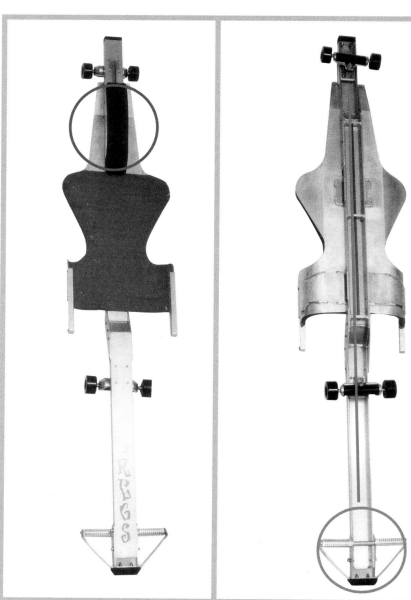

WITH A DECK, WHEELS AND TRUCKS, a street luge is really just a super-modified skateboard. The young sport has different models from different parts of the world, some homemade and others from recently created commercial production lines. The LUGE itself is made of wood, steel or aluminum, and is limited to less than 40 pounds in total and nine feet in length. Various accessories are available to support extended legs, but no aerodynamic fairings or bodywork are allowed. Racers may use any commercially available skateboard-type WHEEL with a hub up to 90 mm in diameter. (At the X Games, all wheels are routinely inspected for their legality.) Some companies are trying to develop a wheel with an aluminum hub that will dissipate heat better and minimize wheel-puking. TRUCKS, also known as AXLES, must be lean-activated like a skateboard and no more than 12 inches wide. For identification, all pilots have a plastic NUMBER PANEL behind their heads. If the number panel is gold, it signifies that the pilot has had high finishes that qualified him as an IGSA (International Gravity Sports Association) Master Racer.

The main piece of protective clothing, aside from a full-face HELMET (known as a *brain bucket*), is a full suit of LEATHERS, of either single- or two-piece construction. As in motorcycle racing, a thick leather skin can do a miraculous job of preventing road rash in the event of a wad. Since rubber-soled shoes are the only legal means of braking, racers use HIGH-TOPS with extra rubber on the bottom. LEATHER GLOVES, custom-adapted for paddling, complete the ensemble.

GOOD TO GO

Luge: $600 to $2,000.
Truck: $50 to $100 apiece.
Wheels: up to $100 for a set of four (bearings extra). Motorcyle road-racing gloves: $40.
Custom-made gloves: $100.
Brain bucket: $150 to S400.
Leathers: $400 to $1,800.

BIKER SHERLOCK A full-on charger despite his long, blond hair and laid-back attitude, Sherlock is the current dominator in all aspects and disciplines of street luge. Heart-stopping passes and barrier-shattering tucks are standard in his repertoire.

RAT SULT This velocity junkie is obsessive about gravity. Sult also unleashed his balls-to-the-wall technique in the snow mountain bike dual speed competition at the '98 Winter X Games.

"BIKER" SHERLOCK

IF THE X GAMES EVER DECIDE TO ADD a multisport competition à la Olympic decathlon, don't bet against Michael "Biker" Sherlock, the San Diegan who has described himself as an "extreme sports junkie." And although his everyday life involves maxing out in one thrill sport after another, including snowboarding, shark diving, motocross and downhill skateboarding, he nearly overlooked street luge. "At first I wasn't interested—I thought it looked lame," he recalls. "But then I got into it." Did he ever. Three golds and a silver later, he's the winningest pilot in X Games history.

In fact, he liked it so much he bought the company—or at least, one of the sanctioning bodies in the fractious sport of street luge, EDI (Extreme Downhill International). But even in a dual role as a competitor and promoter, it's unlikely that Biker will suddenly stop being colorful and outspoken.

"I'm not putting this down," he once said, "because street luge is an extreme thing. But to a lot of these guys, this is the most extreme thing they do, whereas it places sixth or something on my list. I think that gives me an advantage." Number one risky hobby for Sherlock: big-wave surfing. When asked at the '97 Games how he developed such a jump in the paddle apron, he answered, "I don't practice at all, I just surf. All I'm thinking about is getting hit by a big set-wave at Todos [Todos Santos, a monster Baja surf break]—you know, a life-threatening situation. And I just get on out front."

Turning 30, Sherlock now finds himself in the unlikely role of businessman, including ownership of a skateboard company called Dregs. Fortunately, that puts him in a position to address some of the stereotypes that can dog a sport with a renegade reputation. "For one thing," he says, "everyone thinks we're crazy. But just being crazy isn't enough to win the race—you have to have talent."

Biker also has something to say to anyone who dares suggest that, when it comes to being hard core, pros are not bros: "I see articles saying that we as sponsored athletes are sellouts, but that's so wrong. I'm smart if I can do what I love and someone will pay me for it. I am core. I do play all day, but I don't work for some jerk. It's great that the sponsors pay a nice chunk of change, but hey, I made $14,000 last year."

WATER SPORTS

THAT'S GOING OVERBOARD, MAN.

It's weird enough that humans invented internal combustion engines, but then they had to go and invent speedboats. Looking for something even more insane, they started dragging people behind them across the water wearing planks on their feet. Then they jumped. And flipped. And spun. Alas, folks started thinking all of this was "normal." So they blew off the skis. They water-walked backwards, twirled on their booties, jumped face-first, dock-started from towers. Others rode new wake-launched rockets that enabled them to make 10, 20, 30 flights per run. Once everyone agreed that wakeboarding and barefoot jumping had become sufficiently warped beyond all human understanding, they went to the X Games and showed the world what controlled dementia—not to mention a studly set of shoulders—is all about.

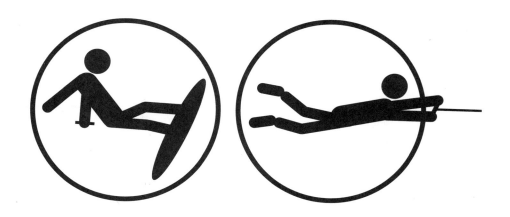

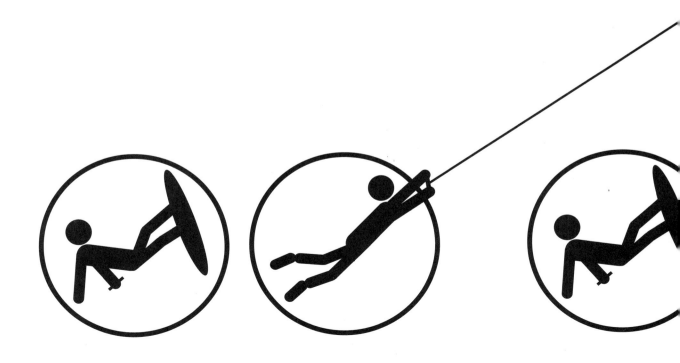

WAKEBOARDING

For all that it owes to the traditions of water skiing, wakeboarding is directly descended from surfing. It was just another one of those things, like skateboarding, that surfers did to maintain their sanity during long periods of wavelessness.

1922 Ralph Samuelson straps two pine boards—eight feet long and nine inches wide— onto his feet and takes off behind a motorboat on Lake Pepin, MN. In a short time, water skiing goes from being a daredevil stunt to a family sport. 1960s Surfers experiment with being towed by boats, and even trucks along the beach. Since they want to be surfing, not water skiing, they develop a variant called "wake surfing"— having a deep-hulled boat achieve the correct speed for maximum wake height, then maneuvering into the critical part of the wave and dropping the rope, thereby surfing an endless wave. 1985 San Diego surfer Tony Finn develops the Skurfer, a hybrid of a water ski and a surfboard. With no straps or bindings, riders concentrate on surf-style carving. Later that year, Finn adds straps to the Skurfer, mirroring a parallel development in Texas, where Jimmy Redmon is working on his Redline brand board. Footstraps permit airs for the first time, and skiboarding, as the young sport is known, begins its divergence from mere flat-water surfing. 1990 ESPN presents the first Skurfer championships on TV, but the sport struggles. Narrow and overly buoyant, Skurfers can only be deep-water-started by strong or very experienced riders. Meanwhile, Redline's designs are light and performance-oriented but lack durability. Things change when Herb O'Brien's H.O. Sports introduces the first compression-molded board, the Hyperlite. Neutrally buoyant, anyone can submerge it for easy deep-water starts. And the phasers (large dimples) on the base break up water adhesion and give the board a quicker, looser feel, plus softer landings from wake jumps. The importance of the wake grows, and the sport becomes increasingly known as wakeboarding. Redmon founds the World Wakeboarding Association. 1992 World Sports & Marketing, a Florida promoter, begins staging pro wakeboard events. 1993 Redmon introduces the now-standard twin-tip design. Instead of a board that goes one direction only, it goes forward and backward equally well. *Wake Boarding* is launched and soon becomes the bible of the sport. 1995 The Pro Wakeboard Series expands, as do the World Wakeboard Championships, with competitors from 17 different countries. 1996 The sport's appearance at the X Games turns on a new generation of fans. Fourteen-year-old Parks Bonifay takes advantage of an injury to long-dominant Darin Shapiro and cops the gold. 1997 There are now 41 wakeboard companies and 1.1 million riders worldwide. Women get their own division at the X Games, which Tara Hamilton takes in a squeaker over the sport's leading lady, Andrea Gaytan.

BAREFOOT JUMPING

The addition of barefoot jumping to the inaugural X Games in 1995 marked a crucial turning point for the sport. It was the first real network TV exposure for the competitive aspect of barefooting, and viewers liked what they saw in this "new" sport. But, crazy as it is, barefooting has been around for a long time.

1947 In Winter Haven, FL, show skier Chuck Sligh theorizes that barefoot skiing might be possible given enough speed, and 17-year-old A.G. Hancock proves him right. Hancock goes on vacation, however, while Dick Pope Jr. duplicates the feat for the media and cops the title as father of barefoot. Let that be a lesson. 1958 Joe Cash invents a deep-water start. 1960s Barefoot remains a novelty act at shows in Florida and Wisconsin, with tricks limited to toe-hold, tumble turn and backward footing. 1963 Australians begin a long period of dominance with their first Barefoot Nationals. 1967 Aussies next pioneer jumping off a water ski ramp. 1973 First international competition in Cypress Gardens. 1977 Louisiana's Bougue Falaya tournament is the first U.S. event to include jumping. Richard Mainwaring is among the first U.K. jumpers. 1978 American Barefoot Club is founded, and first World Championships are held in Canberra. American William Farrell invents sit-down technique called bum-jumping, but Aussie Greg Rees sets the world record at 44 feet. 1979 American Mike Seipel wins his first of seven national barefoot titles. 1985 President of American Barefoot Club seeks to outlaw jumping and fails. 1986 Ron Scarpa gets in *Guinness* by jumping 67 feet from a helicopter, then barefooting away. 1988 Bum-jumping is outlawed. 1990 Mike Seipel accidentally invents inverted jumping. Practicing total relaxation, he lies out face-first, travels extremely far but thinks, I'm going to kill myself, and lets go of the rope. Two jumps later, he skis away. At Nationals, he sets new world record of 72.8 feet. 1991 Seipel shares his technique with Jon Kretchman, who flies 86.3 feet. Now everyone's going invert. 1995 Budweiser Pro Water Ski Tour introduces a new jumping format in which competitors get extra points for prejump tricks. The inaugural X Games follow suit; Aussie Justin Seers edges Ron Scarpa for the overall title. 1996 Germany's Mario Moser jumps 92.9 feet, but Scarpa's superior tricks make him World and X Games champion. 1997 Peter Fleck holds back two South Africans to keep the X Games championship in the U.S.

AIR ROLL A roll performed without using the wake for lift. AIR RALEY The rider hits the wake and allows board and body to swing up overhead while crossing the wake. Rider then swings the board and body down and lands on the downside of the opposite wake. Landed fakie, it's an *Air Krypt*. BACKSIDE ROLL Rider approaches the wake carving heelside, then rolls the board up overhead and lands in the same direction. Off the toeside it's a *Frontside Roll*. BUTTER SLIDE A sideways slide on top of the wake. DOUBLE-UP When a boat U-turns, the double-up is where the wakes meet and create an extra-large ramp. FAKIE Riding backward. HOOCHIE GLIDE An Air Raley with a *heelside* ("method") grab. MOBIUS A Backside Roll with a full twist. ROAST BEEF While performing a two-wake aerial, rider grabs the heel side edge of the board between the legs. S-BEND Rider performs an Air Raley while rotating the body 360 degrees during an invert. SLOB HELI The rider jumps the board off the wake, grabs it toe-side in front of the front foot, then spins 360 degrees to land in forward position. SURFACE 360 Spinning around while remaining on the water. TANTRUM A backflip over the wake.

WINNING AT WAKEBOARDING MEANS PUTTING TOGETHER a string of big tricks that may seem both effortless and improvised. In fact, a lot of planning goes into each performance. Riders first submit an 11-trick list to the three judges, all of whom ride in the boat. With each run consisting of two 25-second passes, riders perform the tricks in order, five per pass with the option of adding the 11th trick in the second pass—usually a big move off the double-up wake. With all aerials, the rider must clear the far wake if the trick is to count. Tricks performed that aren't on the list are called "wild card" tricks and are scored subjectively. Judged on execution, intensity and composition, each run may earn from 0 to 100 points.

Riders also specify boat speed, usually between 18 to 22 mph. Once per round, be it preliminary or final, a rider has the option of dropping the handle before the pass begins if the boat speed is not right. Otherwise, a drop or fall ends that pass.

Many riders use the X Games to debut new tricks, like Parks Bonifay's narrowly missed Double Tantrum in 1997, but these are some of the current favorites.

NO SPORT DESERVES THE EXTREMIST'S ACCOLADE "balls-out" quite like barefoot jumping. Rippled water is just one of the difficulties—even a two-inch chop can pose a real challenge and danger to the jumpers. There was some concern about the Bonita Cove venue at the '97 X Games in San Diego, not only because of the roughness of the harbor but because barefooters are accustomed to freshwater rather than saltwater. Seawater has a different density, and barefooters had trouble adjusting to a surface with what they described as a "softer" feel.

Unlike other pro barefoot competitions, the X Games' format is a unique combination of tricks and distance. The better you air, the more bonus distance is tacked onto your actual flight measurement.

Along with a boat judge, two other officials run the competition. One watches the start and the tricks while the other uses video and computerized tools to monitor distance. There are three components to the judging. The first is the jump itself, including the distance and the success of the rideout, which must continue to a point 210 feet past the jump (good pro jumpers fly at least 65 feet, but the top performances are in the 80-to-90-foot range). The second is how elegantly the jumper goes from the starting move into the correct barefoot position. Some start with a 15-foot drop called a *Tower Start*, while others begin in the water or off the dock.

The third judging component assesses bonus points for tricks, whose planned sequence must be filed with officials beforehand. There is an established system in which each successful trick translates into additional distance. These are some of the tricks to watch for, their distance values and estimated degree of difficulty on a scale of 1 to 10.

0.5 FOOT BONUS

BACK DEEP START A deep-water start lying face-down. **FRONT ONE FOOT. BODY SLIDE** Feet out of water, hands on handle, body sliding along water on one side. **TOWER START**

1.0 FOOT BONUS

TOWER START TO ONE FOOT. BACK FLYING DOCK START Off dock, turn 180 degrees in mid-air, land on the water on the front of the body and then get into regular barefoot position. **TOWER TUMBLE TURN START** Think of a turtle spinning on its back. **180 TURN** Going from frontward to backward, or vice versa. **COMPLETE ONE-FOOT WAKE CROSS**

1.5 FOOT BONUS

FLIP Just what it sounds like. **360 TURN** Complete turn from front to back to front. **BACKWARD ONE-FOOT TOUCH ROPE** Turning 180 degrees and extending one leg behind until it touches the rope. **ONE-FOOT SIDE SLIDE. BACK DEEP ONE-FOOT START** Starting face-down and backwards in the water, then coming up on one foot. **TUMBLE TURN** Curling up and spinning on the surface with shoulders and back. **ONE-FOOT 180 TURN. 180 STEP TURN** Turning around by lifting one leg over the rope. **180 WAKE TURN** About-face while crossing the wake.

WAKEBOARDS HAVE GONE THROUGH A RAPID EVOLUTION in their short history. With lightness and strength being major concerns, most pro WAKEBOARDS are made of aluminum honeycomb or carbon graphite. The flex is important, since delivering a high energy recoil results in greater jumping heights. They also have a TWIN-TIP; in other words, they are symmetrical with a fin at each end so that, with a centered stance, a rider gets equal performance when riding in either forward or switch-stance direction. Dimensions vary, but boards range from 50 to 58 inches in length and are anywhere from 14 to 17.5 inches wide. Wider boards provide more stability and greater lift off the wake, and are thus increasingly the preference of pros. SIDECUT, ROCKER and BOTTOM GROOVES also vary from board to board.

BINDINGS are like rubber shoes, mounted on a metal or plastic base plate that is screwed into the board. Some wakeboarders use straps instead of full bindings. In either case, a tight fit is essential to prevent the rider from falling out during inverted tricks. As for clothes, all that's needed is some BAGGIES and, optionally, a RASH GUARD. Wetsuits are necessary only for cold-water riding.

And of course there has to be a BOAT. At the X Games, competitors use a MasterCraft X-Star wakeboard boat. The rider selects his or her own speed, but it's usually between 18 to 22 mph. The goal is to find the balance of enough speed to generate good forward momentum without being so fast that it flattens out the wake. The only other equipment is the TOW ROPE, made of low-stretch polyurethane in lengths from 45 to 70 feet, and a braided HANDLE with a rubber grip that's wider than the usual water ski version.

FIRST THINGS FIRST, EQUIPMENTWISE: YOU'LL NEED FEET. Contrary to what you'd think, barefooting isn't that hard on the pedal extremities. The heels can get bruised, however, and the way to avoid that is by "skiing" on as much of the foot as possible, rather than plowing through on the heels. And it helps to work up to it. Training in preparation for barefooting is often done with BAREFOOT TRAINERS, boots with a kind of platform underneath. One popular brand of shoe skis, JASKIS, look a lot like high-top clown shoes.

For the TOW BOAT, the X Games uses the MasterCraft outboard BareFoot 200, with a little more punch to reach the 43.6 mph target speed in a hurry. Barefoot boats also need to leave the right sort of trail on the water, consisting of the flat TABLE behind the boat, and the less turbulent CURL on the outside of the wakes where footers prefer to do their tricks. The ROPE is non-stretch polyethylene 75 feet in length, with a HANDLE made of stainless steel or aluminum with a rubber grip, approximately one foot wide.

GLOVES prevent blisters and calluses and improve the grip on the handle, especially important during landing a jump. One brand, Clinchers, is a favorite. HELMETS are mandatory in competition barefoot. Most are plastic with chin strap and foam padding, although some competitors wear full FACE GUARDS. One barefooter, Ray McGallon, took a bad facefall at one point in his career and thereafter wore a Jason-like plastic mask. It's also smart to wear a PADDED WETSUIT that offers a measure of protection against the bruising impact of the water. Made smooth to slice through the water and spin on its surface, they feature padding in the chest, back, ribs, buttocks, thighs and crotch. The chest and rib padding is especially useful in the inverted jumping style favored by the best barefooters. Some jumpers also swear by a BACK SUPPORT BELT.

The RAMP is made of molded fiberglass, a high-tech wonder compared to the linoleum-covered plywood decks propped up on barrels that were standard among the pioneers of the '60s and '70s. Many old-timers remember becoming ramp pizza after mishaps on the makeshift jumps. The modern ramp measures four to five feet wide, 13 feet long, and only 18 inches at the highest point—considerably smaller than a standard water ski jump. Barefoot jumpers are on the ramp for about 2/100ths of a second and launch some 10 to 15 feet in the air.

GOOD TO GO
Padded wetsuit:
$230-$300.
Gloves: $49.
Helmets: $76.
With face guard,
add $30. Rope: $36.
Jump handles: $33.
Trick handles: $66.
Back support:
$45-$100.
Barefoot trainers,
designed by
Ron Scarpa: $129.
Ramp: $2,300.
Boat? If you have to ask. . . .

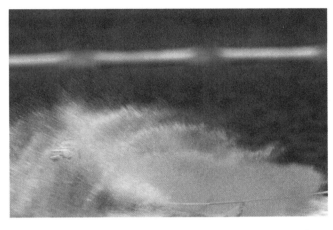

WAKEBOARDING

TARA HAMILTON The new face of women's wakeboarding, this teen has a confident style with the potential to lay it down.

PARKS BONIFAY Spawned into the old-school world of waterskiing, the Kid is defining new-school wakeboarding. You'll need instant replay to truly appreciate his Whirlybirds, Scarecrows and Air Mobiases.

ANDREA GAYTAN The pioneer of women's wakeboarding, she competed head-to-head in '96 against the men. Today she's got to push it hard to stay at the top.

DARIN SHAPIRO The Man. The awards stand was his second home before injury befell him. Now recovered, he blows minds while cranking out gouging bottom turns and executing huge airs.

BAREFOOT JUMPING

PETER FLECK One of the last Americans in a sport being mastered by South Africans, X Games gold eluded him until '97. The fire has been rekindled and Fleck is still hungry.

RON SCARPA The energetic "Raging Bull" was told he was too old to win in '96. He silenced his critics and stood proud at the top of the podium.

A N D R E A   G A Y T A N

LIFE AT THE TOP RULES, EXCEPT FOR ONE NIGGLING DETAIL: everybody's gunning for you. Just ask Andrea Gaytan. Born and raised in Mexico, Gaytan moved to Florida to train for water skiing, but her focus soon switched to wakeboarding. Winning the World Championships in her first week of riding might have helped that decision. Since then, she has dominated the women's division and even came in a respectable 13th in co-ed competition at X Games '96.

Building up to the first all-women's contest at the next X Games, Gaytan battled a flurry of hype insisting that she was washed up and would be dethroned by 15-year-old sensation Tara Hamilton."I feel a lot of people want me to lose," she said before the competition. "It motivates me to show those people who are against me."

With her final run, she thought she'd answered the nay-sayers. "I mean, it was the first time any girl had completed 10 different inverted tricks in one pass, and I was stoked. Tara had fallen on her last trick of her second pass, so I knew I had won." However, the judges ruled that Gaytan had failed to clear the wake with a Half-Cab Roll, and as a result, Hamilton took the gold.

After getting caught on-camera cussing the results, Gaytan and a friend escaped to console themselves with a bottle of Captain Morgan's and a nearby roller coaster. She ended up missing the awards ceremony. And as if all this weren't enough of a career setback, she later suffered an injury that kept her off the water for the entire next winter.

Still, Andrea Gaytan is not about to say *no mas*. She will be back. Only this time, it will be with a bad-girl rep and plenty to prove. "The whole purpose is to win," she says unapologetically. "I don't care for second place."

DARIN SHAPIRO

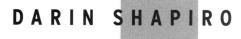

FIFTEEN-YEAR-OLD TARA HAMILTON SHOCKED the wakeboarding nation when she claimed X Games gold in 1997—an astonishing rise to the top for a youngster with less than a year's experience in the sport.

But it was not just any old year. Thanks to a chance meeting, Hamilton had spent those months in the orbit of wakeboarding legend Darin Shapiro, who lives not far from her in Lake Worth, FL. Recognizing Hamilton's background in gymnastics and water skiing—her father was once a three-event competitive skier—Shapiro took the young athlete under his wing.

It's perhaps not surprising that his coaching bore fruit so soon. Before injury struck in 1996, Shapiro had been described as the Michael Jordan of wakeboarding, with a spot permanently reserved atop the medal podium. By focusing on developing Hamilton's skills, however, he was able to distract himself from his own painful rehab. And that too paid off, he says. "I learned about having fun wakeboarding and not getting so mad and critical about everything. It's the same job as before I got hurt, but just more enjoyable."

At the next X Games, Shapiro came back showing more intensity than ever. Although he bobbled some tricks and missed his Speedball (a double frontflip that he invented), he nevertheless did manage to take silver and show the world that he wasn't yet finished as a competitor. Hamilton, meanwhile, made what seemed like an even stronger case for her mentor's future as a coach: she scored the upset victory over Andrea Gaytan that Shapiro had predicted all along.

TARA HAMILTON

PETER FLECK

GO BIG OR GO HOME. It happens to be Peter Fleck's motto, but he took it a bit too literally after failing to stick even one jump in his first two X Games. "Unfortunately, I went home," says the 34-year-old water ski professional from Orlando, FL. At San Diego, however, he finally redeemed himself with clean passes and X Games gold.

It's no surprise that Fleck likes the challenge, the risk, the adrenaline rush of barefooting. But he doesn't necessarily think of it that way. Believe it or not, he says, "It's kind of like golf because you have to be so technical. The timing has to be perfect. But," he adds, and it's a big one, "it's so extreme, it can pound you in a second.

"I'm pretty constantly bruised. I've torn my shoulder, pulled ligaments. I've been knocked out five times from crashes." Nevertheless, he says, "you begin to take the risk for granted. You get comfortable. What you're doing feels safe, whereas it looks really dangerous for others. It's like backseat driving—I'd much rather be in the driver's seat."

Whose courage does Peter Fleck admire? "Guys in the '60s and '70s, they were rock stars. Guys like Mike Body, a big barefooter in '78 and '79."

And then he adds, as if to throw down the gauntlet, "There's not a lot of amp from the younger ranks. In this sport the older generation definitely dominates."

BICYCLE STUNT

KID + BIKE = FREEDOM

The formula has remained the same ever since two-wheel technology first trickled down from the wacky-inventor segment of Adultville. Eventually, a kid had only to jump onto his Stingray in order to leave the dreary shag-rug universe behind. Free to roam the suburban wilderness in menacing packs, he could get down to serious business: a stylish brand of loitering punctuated every now and then by reckless Evel Knievel impersonations, impressing girls and Barneys alike. Parking lots, off-hours shopping plazas and construction-site dirt piles were the new Valhalla. Bent frames and bruised ribs were the new rites of passage. And modern stunt biking? Well, think of it as a grown-up version of the same scene—if you can call groin-threatening stunts like a Candy Bar or a One-Handed Superman grown-up.

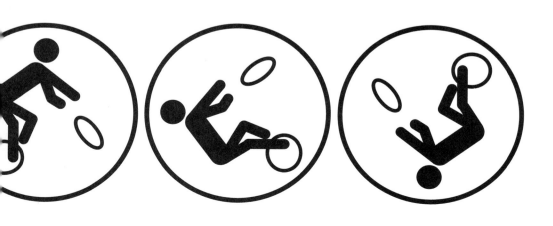

As a competitive sport of its own, bicycle stunt, or freestyle riding, emerged from bicycle motocross (BMX) racing in the early '80s. Dirt courses with numerous jumps were a natural inspiration to more stylish flying. As for Flatland, what else would you expect to develop among suburban kids hanging out 24/7 on their bikes?

1973 The modified Stingray bike, the junior bomber's steed of choice, is replaced by the first official BMX frames. Late '70s/early '80s Racers like Bob Haro (founder of Haro Bikes) discover the skateboard parks that, due to insurance liability issues, have been boarded over and abandoned. Riders break in for illicit sessions in which the first vert and street tricks are developed. 1980 *BMX Action* quotes Cook Bros. Racing's official condemnation of the rogue development: "Our effort is in racing, not 'circus acts.' Furthermore, we feel these stunts should not be exposed to the young riding public." 1982 BMX racing thrives as it enters the American mainstream through its prominent placement in *ET: The Extraterrestrial*. 1983 ESPN presents a seven-race series with six first-place purses of $5,000, one of $15,000 and a grand prize of a car. Meanwhile, Mongoose manufactures the first exclusively freestyle bike. 1984 First freestyle competitions occur in California skateparks. *BMX Action* asks whether stunt could ever overtake BMX in popularity, answering "It's too soon to tell, but one thing's for sure—it's gonna jam!" 1985 Freestyle's first legit year, with an organized competition series. Stunt biking expands well beyond California. 1986 Dennis McCoy begins his Decade of Domination in stunt biking. 1988 Popularity levels out. Previously plush sponsor arrangements decline. Where he once won a truck for his efforts, McCoy would soon see mock prizes like a big old WWF-esque belt. 1995 The first X Games expose bicycle stunt to its largest audience ever. Silver medallist in Dirt, Taj Mihelich, expresses astonishment at seeing stunt biking "hyped up on national TV as the coolest, craziest thing since the Ginsu knife." 1996 Injuries plague stunt riders at the second X Games as tricks get pushed bigger and higher. Matt "The Condor" Hoffman breaks his left foot in three places in Street practice, but he is not to be stopped that easily. Instead, he MacGyvers his shoes by shoving metal strips through the soles and rides his way to his second X Games Vert championship. 1997 As an indication of how well stunt biking has rebounded in popularity, mountain bike manufacturers Specialized and Bontrager begin producing their own BMX bikes.

AT THE X GAMES, STREET AND VERT COMPETITIONS follow the same structure. In each competitive round, both preliminary and final, competitors make two separate runs in randomly determined order. The rider works the ramp and street obstacles for a minimum of 60 seconds and a maximum of 90. If the rider experiences a technical difficulty within the first minute, he will be given two minutes to repair the problem, after which he resumes his run at the time point where he paused.

Five judges assign scores from 70 to 100. Based on the combined average score of all judges and both runs, the top 10 of the initial 20 riders move on to the final, where it's a brand-new competition—the preliminary scores don't carry over. Running in reverse order from tenth to first, the competitors bust another two runs. The winner is the one with the highest average score after all runs are completed.

What gets the judges stoked? Originality, style, flow, variety and amplitude, with big airs obviously the most impressive single factor. Anyone can get three or four feet out of the half-pipe, but the judges want to see who goes eight, nine, 10. (In 1997, English rider Jamie Bestwick won a High Air contest by going 14 feet above the coping. Fellow riders, who at their best max out around 11 feet, called it "sickeningly high.")

On the Street course, the judges want to see riders make use of all the terrain features; the more creatively, the better. They're also looking for a degree of versatility, especially in spinning. Some riders prefer to spin one way. If a competitor can twirl in both directions, the judges will reward the additional difficulty.

For all aerial-oriented bicycle stunt competition, the tricks can be summarized in three categories. There are spinning tricks, rotating anywhere from 180 to 900 degrees, and contortion tricks, where a rider twists his body and the bike, keeping all limbs in place. Then there are limbless variations, in which the rider takes one or both hands and/or feet off the bike, returning them before landing. And you can have virtually limitless combination tricks featuring elements of all three.

What follows is a partial list of lip, spinning and vert tricks with an estimate of their degree of difficulty on a scale of 1 to 10. (Lip tricks are performed at the top edge of a ramp, where a rider either catches his pegs along the coping or stalls on the ledge above it.) Because of the speed with which these tricks are busted and combined, judges don't tabulate degree of difficulty in any scientific way—they simply rely on their expertise to recognize when tricks or trick combinations are exceptionally difficult.

LIP TRICKS

ABUBACA Rider dabs the rear tire on the coping, then descends backwards. **CANADIAN PICK** Front wheel balances on the coping while the back wheel hangs in the air. **DISASTER** After a 180-degree turn in the air, the rider lands on the deck with his rear tire and then continues down the ramp. **DOUBLE PEG GRIND** Both front and rear pegs on one side grind the coping. **FEEBLE GRIND** Front wheel rolls on the deck while the rear peg slides the coping. **FUFANU** The same as an *Abubaca*, except the rider turns 180 degrees to a forward re-entry. **ICE PICK** A momentary point of balance with the rear peg on the coping. If it moves laterally, it's an *Ice Pick Grind*. **MANUAL** Doing a wheelie across the deck before re-entering the half-pipe. **NOSE PICK** Balance point with front wheel on the deck. Add extra points by a coincidental no footer. **NOSE WHEELIE** A Nose Pick that rolls. **SMITH GRIND** A front-peg coping grind with rear wheel on the deck. **TIRE TAP** Balance point with rear wheel on the deck. Make it a *540 Tire Tap* by rotating before going back down. **TOOTHPICK** Balance point with front peg on the coping. **FRAME STAND** Any trick, such as an *Ice Pick*, in which the rider puts one foot on the top tube and stretches the other to the side.

SPINNING TRICKS

A **180** represents the half-turn required to re-enter the ramp forward. In Vert, 180 is the basic air. The other common aerial spins are **360, 540,** 720 and 900. **TAILWHIP** Rider and handlebars remain stationary while the rest of the bike spins fully around. Even more difficult is a TAILWHIP TO ONE HANDER or a DOUBLE TAILWHIP. TRUCK DRIVER A regular 360 combined with a full bar spin. TABLE TOP Rider flattens the bike parallel to the ground. TOBOGGAN Grabbing the seat with one hand, the bars are turned 90 degrees and the butt is hung over the back wheel. X-UP Turning the handlebars one way to the max, then the other.

VERT TRICKS

AIR Straight up the Vert ramp, with a 180-degree turn to re-entry. **BACK FLIP** Rider and bike do the reverse-somersault nasty. On the street course, you land it forward. In the half-pipe, a fakie landing is required. CAN-CAN Rider takes one foot off a pedal, bones it over the top tube and returns to the pedal. CANDY BAR Like the *Can-can*, except the leg thrusts over the handlebars. FAKIE Landing backward in the half-pipe. Difficulty varies from 3 to 8 depending on height. LOOK BACK Rider and bars tweak to face backward. NO FOOTER Legs leave the pedals and scissor wide. Same deal with **NO HANDER, ONE FOOTER** and ONE HANDER. **NO FOOT CAN-CAN** Both feet bone to one side. NOTHING A No Hander and a No Footer done at the same time. **ROCKET AIR** Feet go from pedals to rear pegs and back. **SUPERMAN** Feet leave pedals and rider lays out flat like the Man of Steel. SWITCH HANDER Doing a *One Hander* with the attached hand on the opposite grip.

① ② ③ ④ ⑤ ⑥ ⑦ ⑧ ⑨ ⑩

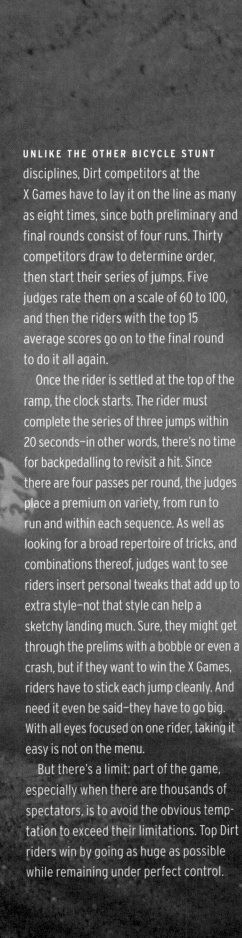

UNLIKE THE OTHER BICYCLE STUNT disciplines, Dirt competitors at the X Games have to lay it on the line as many as eight times, since both preliminary and final rounds consist of four runs. Thirty competitors draw to determine order, then start their series of jumps. Five judges rate them on a scale of 60 to 100, and then the riders with the top 15 average scores go on to the final round to do it all again.

Once the rider is settled at the top of the ramp, the clock starts. The rider must complete the series of three jumps within 20 seconds—in other words, there's no time for backpedalling to revisit a hit. Since there are four passes per round, the judges place a premium on variety, from run to run and within each sequence. As well as looking for a broad repertoire of tricks, and combinations thereof, judges want to see riders insert personal tweaks that add up to extra style—not that style can help a sketchy landing much. Sure, they might get through the prelims with a bobble or even a crash, but if they want to win the X Games, riders have to stick each jump cleanly. And need it even be said—they have to go big. With all eyes focused on one rider, taking it easy is not on the menu.

But there's a limit: part of the game, especially when there are thousands of spectators, is to avoid the obvious temptation to exceed their limitations. Top Dirt riders win by going as huge as possible while remaining under perfect control.

Using only a patch of pavement with no obstacles, the Flatland competition is very much a focused test of rider and bike. Given the two-minute minimum and three-minute maximum at the X Games, it's a long event and you'd better have a huge quiver of moves. Fortunately, as one glimpse of the event will show you, there are an infinite number of ways to trick around on a bike. The goal is to do the hard stuff but make it look easy, to link tricks creatively, and to work every part of the bike and the rider's body. The judges give cookies for style, difficulty, originality/creativity, execution and overall flow. They take cookies away for touches—any time the rider makes contact with the pavement. There are so many tricks in Flatland that they don't even all have names, and new ones are invented all the time. They come in five basic flavors, though: spinning, scuffing, rolling, squeaking and linking.

SPINNING The rider lifts one wheel, then kicks the supporting wheel to start the bike spinning in circles. On the back wheel, it's a MEGASPIN. On the front, a FORKSPIN.

SCUFFING Balanced on one wheel, the rider drags his foot on the tire to move forward or backward. With a FUNKY CHICKEN, the rider rolls backward with his right foot over the cross on the top tube and his left foot on the left front peg. He pulls up on the seat with his right hand and starts to scuff. In a FRONT YARD, the rider starts with his right foot over the bars, then suddenly applies the front brake, steps on the front tire with his right foot, moves his left foot from the pedal to the peg and starts scuffing. Do it without hands and it's called a FREAK SQUEAK.

ROLLING For a HANG 5, the rider stands on the front pegs with the back wheel in the air and rolls forward, either feathering the brakes or not using them at all. In a CLIFF HANGER, the rider starts with a Hang 5 but is sitting on the rear wheel. He then pinches the frame with his knees and lets go of the bar to "hang." A DUMP-TRUCK starts with handlebars backwards and a wheelie with the rider on the back pegs. He grabs on to the right side of the front forks, then lets go of the bars with his left hand and turns the bars 90 degrees, stepping through with his right leg to scuff the rear tire.

SQUEAKING Done mostly on the front wheel, this combines kicking the front tire backward and putting on the brakes. In a PINKY SQUEAK, a rider starts up on the front wheel, kicks the frame and then kicks the back tire backwards. The frame is spinning now and the rider steps over it, using one foot to kick the tire while the other steps off and back on to a peg. To add difficulty, a rider can stand on the pedals instead of the pegs, which in this case would result in a PEDAL PINKY SQUEAK.

LINKING A rider creatively joins tricks in sequence. In a BOOMERANG, a rider rolls slowly forward, feet on the back pegs, and swings the right leg forward, then backward for momentum. While pushing off the left peg with the left foot, the rider jumps around the head tube, traveling 180 degrees and carving in an arc. For a BARHOP, he jumps over the bars while keeping the pedals level and rolling slowly forward.

The Condor's geometry :
Head tube angle – 74 degrees
Seat tube angle – 65 degrees
Bottom bracket height – 11 $\frac{3}{8}$ inches
Wheelbase – 36 inches to 37 $\frac{1}{2}$ inches
Chainstay length – 14 $\frac{1}{2}$ inches to
15 $\frac{3}{4}$ inches
Top tube length – 20 $\frac{3}{4}$ inches

The durability and quality of Matt Hoffman's custom-designed Condor created a new standard in freestyle bicycles. A Toys Я Us bike has 36 spokes, a 43-tooth sprocket and tires handling air pressure up to 45 PSI. The Condor has 48 SPOKES, a bigger SPROCKET and beefier TIRES designed to withstand air pressure of 120 PSI. Hoffman's WHEEL RIMS are twice as thick to prevent dings on the vert ramp when riding the coping. The REAR AXLE is 14 mm instead of 3/8 of an inch because the PEGS are mounted directly onto it. The SEAT is kicked back to give more room up front. Price: $700.

FREESTYLE RIDERS ARE NOT concerned with excess poundage. Whereas a mountain bike weighs around 22 lbs., a STUNT BIKE weighs 30 to 35 lbs. Because Flatland bikes don't even need to get off the ground, but still need to hold a rider's weight in unpredictable ways, they are heavier still, around 35 to 40 lbs. FRAMES basically come in small, medium or large sizes, but all freestyle bikes have the same 20-inch WHEELS. Stunt bikes have both front and back BRAKES. One special feature is a device called a GYRO, just below the stem, which permits the handlebars to spin without tangling up the brake cables. Flatland riders also use "free coaster" brakes that allow the wheels to move backwards without using the pedals. In order to do certain lip tricks in Vert, or to grind along bars in Street or support a rider in Flatland, freestyle bikes have steel or aluminum PEGS which thread onto front and rear axles. They stick out about three or four inches from the wheel.

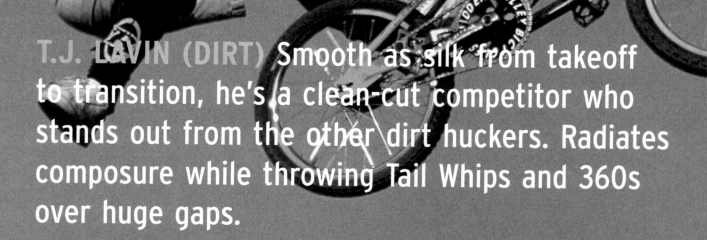

T.J. LAVIN (DIRT) Smooth as silk from takeoff to transition, he's a clean-cut competitor who stands out from the other dirt huckers. Radiates composure while throwing Tail Whips and 360s over huge gaps.

RYAN NYQUIST (DIRT & STREET) At 18, this trail rider turned insane and blasted into the bike stunt series. Outgoing, amped, rock solid, he confidently links back-to-back 360s and 360 bar spins.

DAVE MIRRA (VERT & STREET) Singlehandedly changing the performance levels of stunt biking, Miracle Boy is incredibly smooth with a bag of untouchable tricks.

DENNIS MCCOY (VERT & STREET) At 30, he shows no signs of letting up. Solid, light on his feet, in complete control, McCoy feeds off Dave Mirra and vice versa.

MATT HOFFMAN (VERT) For years, the undisputed "King of Vert," but the years of pushing the envelope are starting to catch up with him. But what a legacy—this adrenaline junkie pulled off moves at 18 that the current crew of brash riders still can't emulate.

TREVOR MEYER (FLATLAND) Focused. Obsessive. Innovative. New school. The fluid Meyer is miles ahead of the other flatlanders.

DAVE MIRRA

YOU MAY REMEMBER SEEING A MAGAZINE AD for BOKS showing Dave "Miracle Boy" Mirra next to Matt "The Condor" Hoffman, with a caption that reads, "Having their spleen removed isn't the only thing they have in common." Like Hoffman, Mirra is an airgod with a string of top finishes behind him. And although he took silver to the Condor's gold at both the '95 and '96 X Games Vert competition, he rebounded to take the '97 event. Meanwhile, the 24-year-old has yet to post anything but a first-place finish in X Games Street.

For the New York State native, who now makes his home in North Carolina, bikes and stunting were a constant feature of growing up. Mirra still trains hard to achieve his judge-stoking trademark: making hard tricks look easy and linking with uncanny smoothness.

As for the spleen incident, Mirra was riding in a Hoffman-organized event in Texas after the '95 X Games when, he recalls, "I was doing a look-back on Vert, and my shirt got tangled in the handlebars. I went down hard and tore my spleen in half." Fortunately, the Condor had already suffered a similar injury and had Mirra diagnosed in the ambulance on the way to the hospital.

No wonder Mirra relaxes with safe activities like golf, chess, darts and pool. And when he's not riding, he'll kick back and study video tapes of his own sick performances. "It's kind of weird," says Miracle Boy, "because it always looks a lot harder than it feels."

MATT HOFFMAN

THE CHARISMATIC LEADER OF THE FREESTYLE RENAISSANCE, Matt "The Condor" Hoffman did it with a two-pronged attack: by shattering the limits of gravity as a competitor and, at the same time, shoving the industry forward as both a manufacturer and event organizer.

At the age of 15 Hoffman got kicked out of school for missing too many days to go to the amateur competitions where he routinely destroyed the field. A pro at 16, three years later he left his sponsor and did the unthinkable: he bought a semi-truck that he was too young to drive legally, threw a ramp in the back and started touring as Hoffman Promotions. Then he branched out into a second business, Hoffman Bikes. And when frame-builders failed to keep up with his demand, he defied conventional wisdom and started Hoffman Manufacturing. All this before he was old enough to walk into a bar and really start acting like a businessman.

Recently contracted to organize events well into the future for ESPN, Hoffman has also taken up film-making. Of course, when it came time to create a feature-length video with his team, who better to write, produce and edit than Hoffman himself? The final product was well received, but there were a few sketchy moments: "I dressed the guys up in really bad outfits and made them act," he said. "I anticipated the team quitting on me."

They haven't. Nor has The Condor quit on them. His riding remains strong, despite telling the press before X Games '97 that "I'm sort of out of the whole competition thing—only when I really get a hair up it do I need to compete." He must have had one in San Diego, where he shook off the rust and copped third to follow his previous two consecutive golds in Vert.

Nevertheless, you should expect Hoffman's biggest future achievements to be as a tycoon. He certainly has the credentials. "I'm a big candidate for an ulcer," he admits. "Too much stress, alcohol and spicy food."

DENNIS MCCOY

ALL PRO ATHLETES DREAM OF LEAVING A LASTING impression on their chosen field. Only in their wildest dreams, however, could they hope to match Dennis McCoy's contribution to freestyle bicycling. A clean-cut rider who became the sport's first non-Californian star, he will forever be acknowledged for what's now known as his Decade of Domination, a spectacular competitive rampage beginning in 1986.

On the eve of the sport's final competition of 1995, McCoy had won a previous nine straight overall titles. "There was a lot of hype on that 10th year, and a lot of people weren't sure I'd get it," he recalls. People noticed that he'd been concentrating on ramps and slacking off in Flatland, and he was second overall going into the finals. But while others were out partying that weekend, he stayed to practice in the hotel parking lot. Sure enough, he went on the next day to top the bicycle stunt world for an astounding tenth year.

Now in his early 30s, McCoy remembers starting out on a "K-Mart special" his parents bought him in the late '70s. That soon led to BMX bike racing, then freestyle comps in 1984. He says he's ridden a bicycle every day since he was 13, and has remained remarkably healthy doing it. True, there have been setbacks—he once broke his jaw two days before the full-face helmet he'd ordered arrived in the mail—but McCoy claims that "it's way, way safer than it appears to be." Still, he wears plenty of armor, including a chest protector.

Dues all paid up, McCoy now enjoys playing elder statesman in the sport, whether it's designing frames for his new sponsor, K2, or fighting City Hall when it wanted private ramps torn down in his hometown of Kansas City. He plans to continue competing, although without the added pressure of history: the "overall" category has been taken out of bicycle stunt competition. "I'm off the hook," says Dennis McCoy, keenly aware of the pack of hungry and talented young riders nipping at his Airwalks. "It's now become next-to-impossible to place top five in everything."

TREVOR MEYER

Trevor Meyer's Dyno Slammer, made by GT, employs a system called ORYG, which detangles the rear brake cables, an important component in flatland. The FRONT-BACK BRAKES are used 90 percent of the time to better balance freestyle tricks. Just below and in front of the seat is an additional STANDING PLATFORM used for standing and balancing tricks, along with the AXLE PEGS. The SEAT is kicked back to create more room for maneuvering. Durability? Put it this way. The military uses the same material for the underbody of their STOL (*short takeoff and landing*) planes that GT uses in their bikes. Price: $830.

THE DEBUT OF THE FLATLAND COMPETITION AT THE '97 X GAMES raised a prickly question. With its largest-ever television audience looking on, would this tamer, more finesse-oriented discipline be able to compete with the flash of the rowdier events? Rider after rider provided convincing evidence that it could. But the verdict—Flatland rocks!—was assured when Trevor Meyer hammered a complex but flawless routine that made the crowd literally hold its breath, fearing for a touch of the pavement that never came.

No wonder they call him The Machine. Meyer's precision and showmanship were honed by several seasons spent electrifying NBA halftime audiences in exhibitions with his GT crew. Obviously, at a gig like that, the last thing you want to do is come off looking lame. The pressure of being part of "Showtime" turns out to be an ideal training ground for dialing in perfection at finals time.

When not bunking at the team house in Huntington Beach, CA, Meyer lives with his mother in Spring Park, MN. Obviously, Mom's cool: part of Meyer's success stems from the fact he learned how to do a lot of his tricks in the living room. When he got too close to the walls, it forced him to invent a lot of variations as he backed off. Among the many techniques he's invented, backward scuffing is one of the most impressively difficult.

Where the sport goes now is largely up to Meyer. As *Ride BMX* once wrote: "It's fun to pretend that Trevor Meyer is an unstoppable flatland robot here to single-handedly take over the planet and initiate his own New World Order." Hey, who needs to pretend?

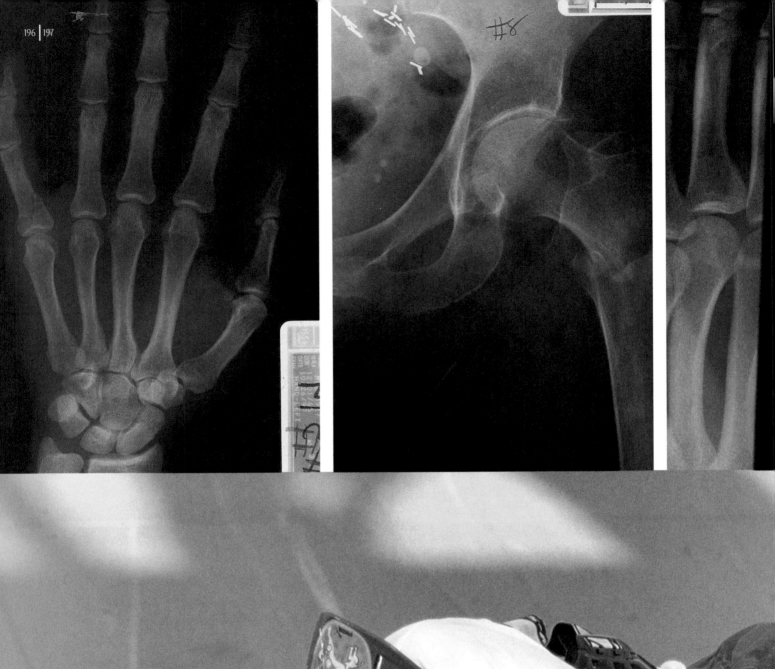

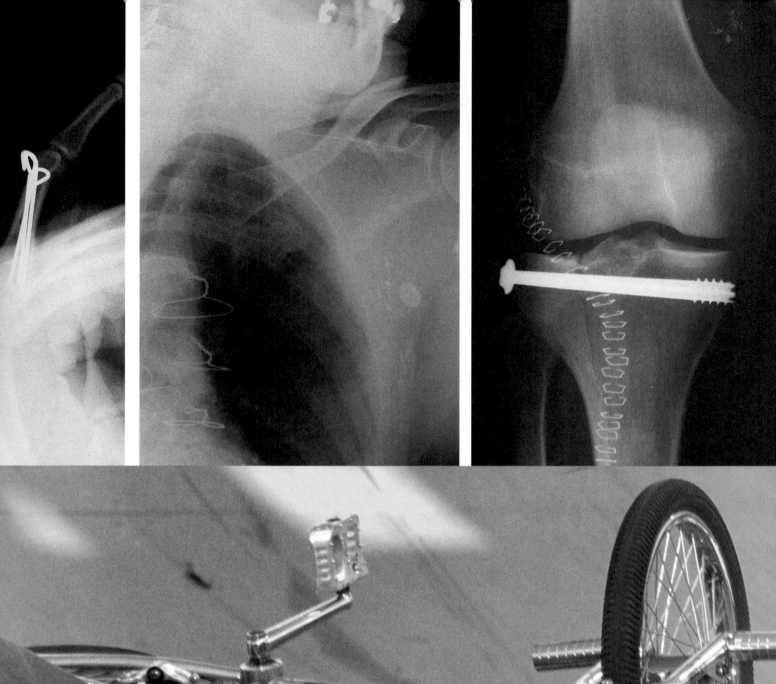

SPORTCLIMBING

NO BILLBOARD TATTOOS, NO WILD KINGDOM PIERCINGS, NO SUPERFLY THREADS.

At first glance, sportclimbing appears to be the white sheep of the X Games. Scratch deeper, however, and you'll find plenty in common with other factions of the new sports tribe. Add it up: Climbers, for example, are every bit as serious about hangin' with their friends—they just take it to absurdly literal lengths. Likewise, they make the impossible look easy and are often considered insane by non-believers. Their little mistakes involve orthopedic surgeons; their big ones tempt the Grim Reaper. When not simply understanding one another with wordless, near-telepathic communication, they speak a language incomprehensible to outsiders. And the hard-rock hardcore is addicted to the same adrenaline cocktail as the other X Gamers. Theirs just happens to be heavily spiked with lactic acid.

Regardless of who you think our ancestors were, scrambling up trees and rocks has been a key to survival for a long time. As for the date of the first climbing competition, that is not known, but they've been taking place in Eastern Europe for at least 60 years.

MID-1800s Sportclimbing's roots connect directly to the European Alps, the first place anyone climbed mountains strictly for fun. Peak ascents satisfy a romantic urge to experience nature while taming it. The first great summit expeditions take the easiest routes, but as they are done and re-done, European mountaineers begin to seek more challenging climbs. 1900 Sheer cliffs are considered for the first time. "Body belay" techniques are developed so one climber can hold onto the other in the event of a fall. 1910 Alpinists are further aided by the invention of steel carabiners and pitons that can be fixed to a cliff. This leads to the handy descent technique called "rappelling": Austrians and Germans lead the charge. The British, meanwhile, lacking big-wall mountains of their own, start the "training" sport of rock climbing practiced as an end in itself. LATE 1920s Lagging behind, America is finally introduced to roped climbing. 1939 World War II interrupts sportclimbing's progress, but it provides a great technical bonus: the development of lightweight aluminum carabiners as well as nylon ropes with greater elasticity or "give" than traditional hemp. 1950s A hot climbing scene emerges in California's Yosemite Valley, with ever more daring big-wall ascents that include "aid" climbing–placing holds and using ropes on faces that would otherwise be unclimbable. The British tend to disparage this new technique, holding to a purist ethic called "free climbing," using ropes only for protection. It is this branch of alpinism that now includes sportclimbing. 1960s Tight-fitting high-top sneakers replace lug-soled boots as the shoe of choice for Americans, who by now have joined their transatlantic colleagues in the free climbing quest. In California, French expatriate Yvon Chouinard, founder of Patagonia, devises new forms of protection such as aluminum nuts and spring-loaded cams. Faster, lighter climbs are the result. 1982 "Sticky rubber" is introduced, offering greatly improved friction and a tool for skyrocketing difficulty levels in free climbing. 1985 The first organized international competition takes place on outdoor cliffs near Bardonecchia, Italy. Purists protest bitterly, and some loudly boycott the event. But it's of little use: competitive sport climbing is here to stay. 1988 A world organizing body is founded. The next year, the first World Cup competition in the U.S. takes place at Snowbird, Utah. At the time, there is one climbing gym in the entire country. (Currently there are around 400). 1995 At the inaugural X Games, international competition returns to U.S. soil for the first time in four years. Robin Erbesfield wins the Combined Bouldering and Difficulty event, while fellow American Hans Florine takes Speed, serving notice that U.S. competitors are getting over a long inferiority complex. 1996 More good news for U.S. climbing: 15-year-old Katie Brown takes the first of two consecutive X Games Difficulty competitions. 1997 Brown is joined on the podium by fellow wunderkind Chris Sharma, showing that a new generation of climbers is ready to take on the world.

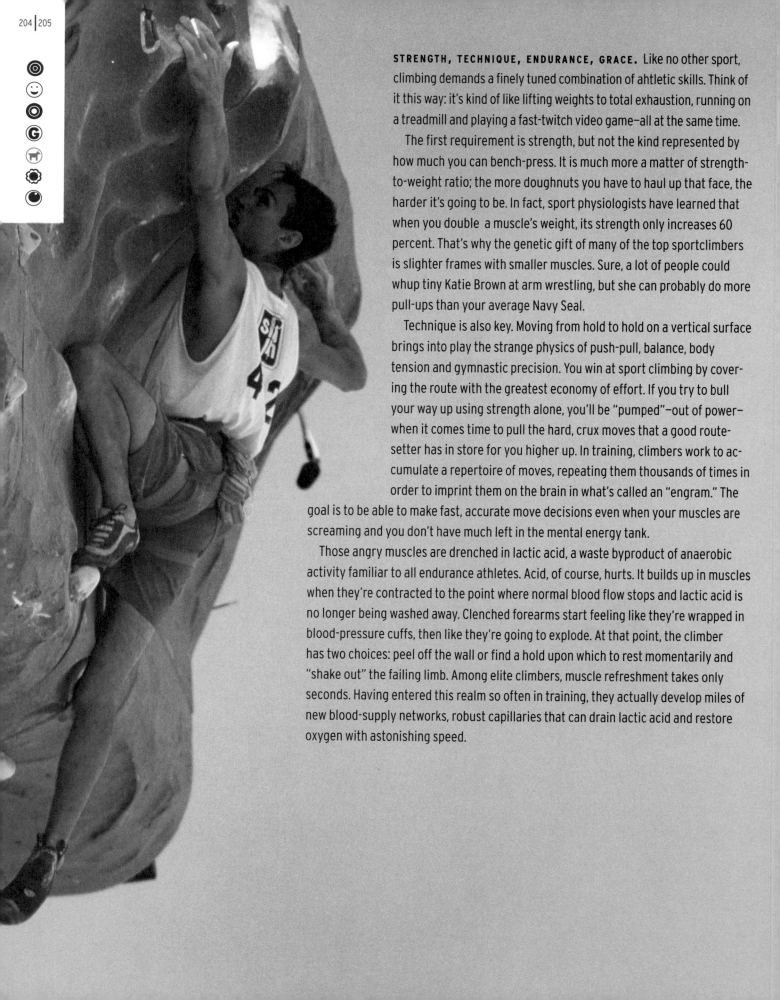

STRENGTH, TECHNIQUE, ENDURANCE, GRACE. Like no other sport, climbing demands a finely tuned combination of ahtletic skills. Think of it this way: it's kind of like lifting weights to total exhaustion, running on a treadmill and playing a fast-twitch video game—all at the same time.

The first requirement is strength, but not the kind represented by how much you can bench-press. It is much more a matter of strength-to-weight ratio; the more doughnuts you have to haul up that face, the harder it's going to be. In fact, sport physiologists have learned that when you double a muscle's weight, its strength only increases 60 percent. That's why the genetic gift of many of the top sportclimbers is slighter frames with smaller muscles. Sure, a lot of people could whup tiny Katie Brown at arm wrestling, but she can probably do more pull-ups than your average Navy Seal.

Technique is also key. Moving from hold to hold on a vertical surface brings into play the strange physics of push-pull, balance, body tension and gymnastic precision. You win at sport climbing by covering the route with the greatest economy of effort. If you try to bull your way up using strength alone, you'll be "pumped"—out of power—when it comes time to pull the hard, crux moves that a good route-setter has in store for you higher up. In training, climbers work to accumulate a repertoire of moves, repeating them thousands of times in order to imprint them on the brain in what's called an "engram." The goal is to be able to make fast, accurate move decisions even when your muscles are screaming and you don't have much left in the mental energy tank.

Those angry muscles are drenched in lactic acid, a waste byproduct of anaerobic activity familiar to all endurance athletes. Acid, of course, hurts. It builds up in muscles when they're contracted to the point where normal blood flow stops and lactic acid is no longer being washed away. Clenched forearms start feeling like they're wrapped in blood-pressure cuffs, then like they're going to explode. At that point, the climber has two choices: peel off the wall or find a hold upon which to rest momentarily and "shake out" the failing limb. Among elite climbers, muscle refreshment takes only seconds. Having entered this realm so often in training, they actually develop miles of new blood-supply networks, robust capillaries that can drain lactic acid and restore oxygen with astonishing speed.

DIFFICULTY

Difficulty is the first of two events for both men and women in X Games sportclimbing competition. There is one final route, which competitors are prevented from seeing beforehand by being placed in isolation. Runs must be less than 10 minutes during preliminaries, less than 11 in semifinal, and less than 12 during the final. Scores are computed based on the number of holds reached, with additional points as follows: Let's say the climber just barely touches hold number 39 before peeling off the wall—that's 39 points. Touching and controlling, however, is worth 39.1, while touching, controlling and advancing yields 39.2 points. The maximum route score—the hold's value plus one point—is given when the climber reaches the highest hold and clips into the carabiner. If a tie occurs, a countback procedure determines who got more points in the semifinal round, or the preliminaries if necessary.

SPEED

Two nearly identical routes are set on the wall and 20 competitors post a time on each by reaching and triggering a clock-stopping button at the top. Climbers with the top eight combined times then meet head-to-head in seeded, bracketed competition. To ensure that neither climber benefits from an easier route, competitors switch sides for a second run. Best combined time advances. Disqualifications occur for touching anything beyond the boundary of the route, for committing two false starts or for using prohibited holds or protection points.

THE SUCCESS OR FAILURE OF ANY SPEED OR DIFFICULTY COMPETITION rests on the skill of the routesetters. It sounds simple enough: The routesetter selects artificial holds of various shapes and sizes, then solidly attaches them to the wall. (A "spinning" or loose hold is cause for a technical incident, allowing a climber to start over.) The route is meticulously designed to pose a precise series of problems—and to prevent climbers from choosing easier variations through the sequence. Route-setters climb and reclimb the route to ensure that there is only one "good" way to execute a sequence, while also putting up decoy holds that will dead end or just tire out a competitor who misreads the wall. Just before the competition begins, chalk is rubbed on every hold so that the "good" route doesn't stand out. If more than one person is able to make it up the wall, that means a tie—the worst possible result.

All of the X Games routesetting has been done by Mike Pont, Tony Yaniro and Robyn Erbesfield. In the early '90s, Pont and Yaniro became the first Americans to get international certification by the climbing world's governing body, the UIAA Union International des Associations d'Alpinisme. Back in 1978, Yaniro put up the hardest route in the world at the time, Grand Illusion (5.13c), which *Climbing* called a "visionary test piece." In 1995, they established the American League of Forerunners to organize and improve routesetting.

After winning the World Cup from 1991 to 1995, Robyn Erbesfield retired as America's most successful competitive climber. Since then she has concentrated on routesetting, showing the same dedication that she brought to competing.

Anybody who would come up with a complex numerical system to describe how difficult routes are is obviously very specific about descriptions. It's only natural that climbers would also use a jargon as vast and colorful as any at the X Games.

BETA Information about how a route should be climbed, what holds to look for, what body position works best and so on. In climbing competitions, contestants are kept in isolation areas so they won't gather visual beta from watching other competitors. Also, spectators are specifically warned not to shout beta advice to friends on the wall. BETA FLASH Flashing a route while armed with crucial bits of information on how to do *crux* moves (see below), often by being "talked through" by someone on the ground. BOMBER Short for *bombproof*, any hold that is extremely solid and easy to use. A piece of *protection* can also be called *bomber*. BRAIN BUCKET A helmet, useful in outdoor climbing principally as a guard against loose bits of rock falling from above. CAMPUS Moving from hold to hold, while the legs dangle free. Comes from *campus board*, a wooden training device with small ledges that are used to train finger strength and dynos. CHEESE GRATER Falling and scraping down a slab. CLIP To pull the rope up and snap it into the carabiner. Competitors must make all the clips on a given route—they're not allowed to skip any no matter how strong they're feeling. CRATER Hit the ground. CRUX The trickiest point in a climb; the most likely spot for a climber to be spit off. DECK The ground, or, as a verb, hitting the ground. FLASH Both noun and verb, it means getting to the top on the first attempt without falling. GREASE Not being able to hold on; slipping off something. GRIPPED Paralyzed with fear. MANKY The opposite of *bomber*. MUNGE Dirt or vegetation found in cracks or pockets. Usually must be cleaned before the climber attempts to use the hold. OVERHANG Any part of a wall that is beyond vertical; that is, getting closer to being a ceiling than a wall. PRO Short form of *protection*, the various devices to which carabiners are fixed. PUMPED When a climber's arms are flooded with lactic acid and the consequent pain. A really steep, exhausting climb is *pumpy*. RAD Occasionally used slang referring to sportclimbing, as in *Trad* vs. *Rad*. ROOF A serious overhang, more or less parallel to the ground. SCREAMER A big fall. SEND Finish a route. SEWING MACHINE LEGS After a long time standing on a small hold, or in a particularly awkward position, a climber's legs may start to shake uncontrollably. Also called *Elvis Syndrome*. SLAB A wall that is less than vertical. SHORT ROPING When a belayer doesn't give a leader enough rope to make a clip and the leader has to pull up more rope. Can pull a climber off the wall. TAKE A command to the belayer to get ready to take the climber's full weight. In other words, Help, I'm falling! WHIPPER A fall.

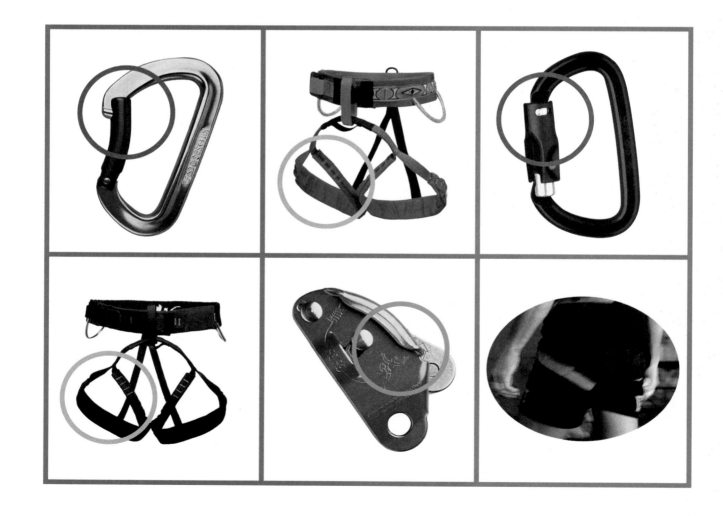

COMPARED TO TRADITIONAL CLIMBING, which can require a climber to carry along everything from an axe to a parka to an electric drill, sportclimbing is a streamlined affair. Since PROTECTION, usually in the form of BOLT HANGERS, is already fixed to the wall, you'll only need a few items. Remember, though, this sport is not about just grabbing whatever gear and giving it a whirl: you should only consider learning it in a trusted setting with proven equipment.

A HARNESS is made up of a waist belt and leg loops that girdle the mid-section. A ROPE, attached to the harness, is clipped into protection. Ropes come in at least 55-meter lengths, made from synthetic fibers in a core bundle of strands with a protective braided outer sheath. They are said to be "dynamic" in that they will stretch to absorb the shock of the climber's weight during a fall. A BELAY DEVICE is a friction-based metal contraption that routes the rope so that the belayer can pay out slack as the climber rises, but easily apply the brakes in the event of a fall. The next essential is an array of CARABINERS, oval or D-shaped loops of aluminum alloy with a hinged or locking gate on one side. In competition sportclimbing the climber doesn't have to carry his or her own. They're already preplaced and ready to clip into two carabiners attached to a bolt by a piece of nylon webbing called a QUICKDRAW.

Advances in CLIMBING SHOE technology have helped advance the sport. They are pointy, rigid and cruelly tight, since they're worn up to two sizes too small. Their "sticky rubber" soles allow a climber to smear against the slightest protuberance on the rock and gain enough purchase to move on. The only other personal gear you'll need, aside from some light, unencumbering clothing, is a CHALK BAG, a small pouch clipped to the back of the harness. It contains powdered gymnastic chalk that keeps fingers dry and grippy during the climb.

GOOD TO GO

Carabiner: $10-$17.
Harness: $62-$90.
Belaying device: $70.
Adjustable helmet: $70-$75.
Shoes: $100-$150.
Rope: $100-$160,
depending upon diameter,
material and impact force.

CHRIS SHARMA (DIFFICULTY) Cool and confident, this teen possesses uncanny route-setting insight. The secret to his preternatural success: Focus.

FRANÇOIS LEGRAND (SPEED) World champion in '91, '93 and '95, Legrand is not getting any slower, the competition is simply getting faster.

HANS FLORINE (SPEED) Undefeated in Speed competition, he's a proven champion across the globe, including victories in all three X Games (in '96, he was recovering from dysentry). Maniacally quick, tremendously fit, walls appear horizontal when attacked by "Hollywood" Hans.

CHRIS BLOCH (SPEED) The pressure of competing against Florine would break anyone else, but the challenge only makes Block more determined to bull ahead of "Hollywood" Hans. Called an "indoor phenomenon" by *Climbing*, he's an instructor at City Rock in San Francisco.

KATIE BROWN (DIFFICULTY) Shy on the ground, merciless in ascending a Difficulty route. Mature and precise, Brown is at the head of the class in the new school of climbers.

ELENA OVTCHINNIKOVA (SPEED & DIFFICULTY) The daughter of a champion climber, the versatile Russian is also a mother herself, rebounding from pregnancy stronger and faster than ever.

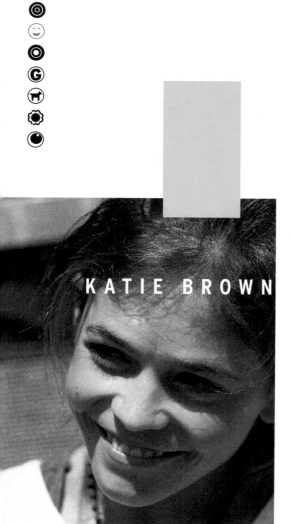

KATIE BROWN

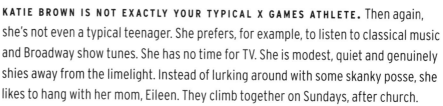

KATIE BROWN IS NOT EXACTLY YOUR TYPICAL X GAMES ATHLETE. Then again, she's not even a typical teenager. She prefers, for example, to listen to classical music and Broadway show tunes. She has no time for TV. She is modest, quiet and genuinely shies away from the limelight. Instead of lurking around with some skanky posse, she likes to hang with her mom, Eileen. They climb together on Sundays, after church.

But at five feet, 85 pounds, Brown is the dynamo of dyno, a climber blessed with an astonishing ratio of strength-to-weight, dazzling grace and an unflappable psyche that together have made her the toast of the vertical set. What's even more remarkable is the short time it's taken to reach that pinnacle.

Brown started climbing only in 1993, when she was 13. At first the sport didn't make much of an impression. "I don't really remember," she says of her first sessions, "but obviously I liked it right away, because I kept doing it." Indeed. Just two years later she won her age group at the Junior Nationals, and a few months after that, came in fourth in full-fledged Nationals. That was the last time she finished anywhere but on top at that level of competition.

At the '96 X Games, Brown had her first competitive exposure to the world's best climbers. The crowd was buzzing about the 15-year-old sensation, and she didn't disappoint. She was the only woman to flash the 5.13a final route in Difficulty, taking gold ahead of Laurence Guyon, who was ranked number two in the World Cup series, and European champion Liv Sansoz. It also made her the youngest woman in history to win in elite international competition.

The next year saw her leave her Georgia home to follow the professional climbing circuit, with her mother to help keep her feet on the ground—as if she needed it. Brown came into the '97 X Games as the favorite—equipped, as she is for every competition, with her Bible, flute and teapot.

Unsurprisingly, she flashed. And won. And said very little about it. If there's any part of Katie Brown that feels like pumping her fist and shouting, Wicked! it hasn't yet emerged. It probably never will.

CHRIS SHARMA

OF ALL THE SPORTS WHERE THE MAN IS, WELL, A BOY, you wouldn't expect it in the strength-and-savvy world of sportclimbing. But that's the way it is with Chris Sharma, who got vertically addicted at the age of 11 after visiting his first climbing gym, City Rock, in Berkeley, CA. When an indoor wall opened in his hometown of Santa Cruz, he soon gained fame as the local grom who was climbing super-difficult 5.12 in his first year. Older climbers watched in awe. When they met Sharma and determined that he was indeed a cool kid, they started encouraging him to explore his obvious gift. They'd make problems for him to solve. One of them was a reach move on what they called "the Sharma-proof Roof." Needless to say, it didn't stay that way for long.

Since then, Sharma has emerged as nothing less than one of the world's top climbers, as at home in the gym as he is on big mountain walls. Among his difficult first ascents was Necessary Evil at the Virgin River Gorge in Arizona—the hardest grade in the U.S. at 5.14c (the "c" is part of the Yosemite Decimal System, which ranks a wall's grade from 5.0 to 5.10, then 5.10a, 5.10b, 5.10c, 5.10d, 5.11a, 5.11b and so on).

As a competitor, he made a quick transition from totally dominating age-group events to kind of dominating open events. In his first X Games appearance in 1996, he was headed for the finals and a much-anticipated showdown between the veteran Europeans and the gangly 15-year-old American upstart. Forced to bail when a hold spun during warm-up, badly spraining his wrist, he didn't get to face the world's elite until the next year at the World Championships in Paris. Despite climbing two holds higher than Francois Petit, Sharma placed second: European climbing comps require only that you touch a hold, not control it as you must in the U.S. Petit was able to lunge and slap a higher hold.

At the '97 X Games, however, there were no errors due to inexperience—he took gold decisively in the Difficulty event. Along with Katie Brown, Chris Sharma served notice that a new generation of American climbers has reached the summit.

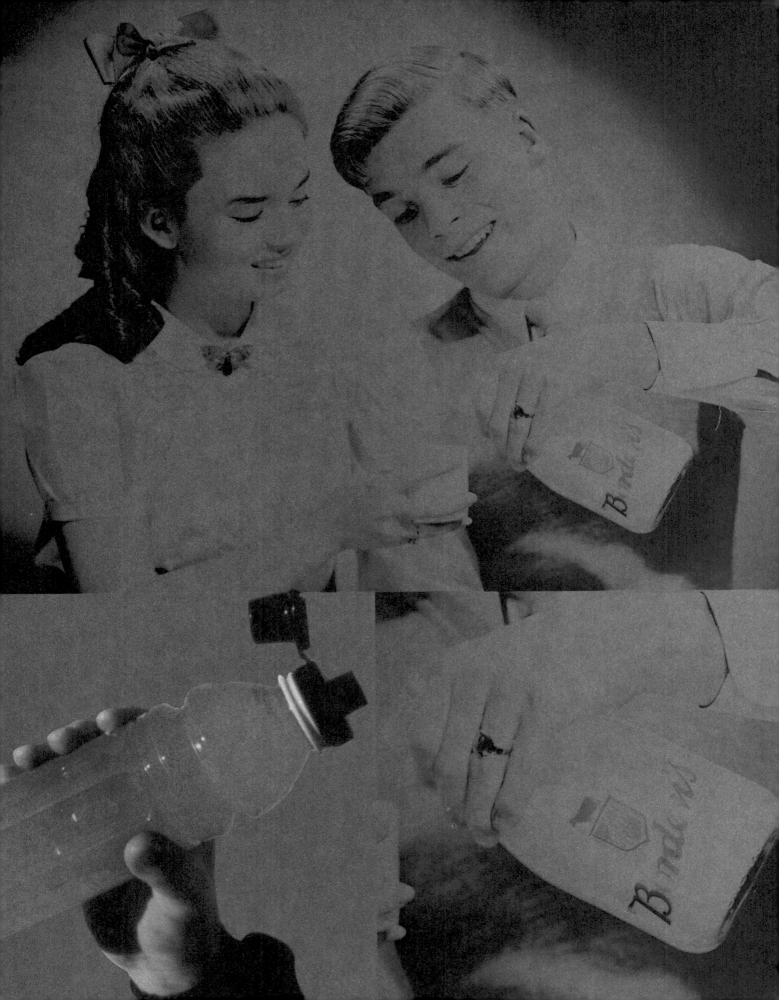

BIG AIR SNOWBOARDING

HUCK NOW: AVOID THE RUSH.

People asked, Why have big air snowboarding in the summer X Games? Apart from the rhetorically obvious *Why not?*, there is a three-part answer: *(a)* Because we can, *(b)* Because it totally rips and *(c)* Who said snowboarding is limited to winter? Half-pipes carved into permanent snowfields have for years made summer snowboard camps the breeding ground for the hottest young riders and, most importantly, the sickest huckers on snow. In San Diego in '97, thanks to a miracle called liquid nitrogen, the folks at the beach got a first-hand opportunity to learn that there's nothing like a house-sized kicker, a sunny day and an XXL posse to provoke hours of spine-snapping fun. Don't try this at home? If only, dude.

In less than a decade, snowboarding has grown from a sport featuring a few stubborn, opinionated iconoclasts who had to beg for access to resort chairlifts, to a multimillion-dollar industry with rock star luminaries pushing the fashion mainstream. How prescient, the 1966 advertisement proclaiming that surfing on snow "is indeed a classic winter alternative . . . Truly a breakthrough in winter sports equipment . . . A new perspective in downhill thrills."

1963 For his eighth-grade shop project, Californian Tom Sims modifies a skateboard deck so it will slide on snow. **1965** Across the continent, inventor Sherman Poppen notices his daughter trying to stand on her sled while riding downhill. He goes into the garage, attaches a pair of snow skis, adds a rubber mat and a rope attached to the tip for steering and gives it to her as a Christmas present. **1966** Calling it the "Snurfer," Poppen puts a version of that prototype into production. He eventually sells hundreds of thousands through toy and sporting goods stores, infecting North America with the urge to surf on snow. Snurfer acolytes begin to organize riding contests. **1969** Bob Weber's Skiboard features the first bindings. **1970** Inspired by kids sliding on cafeteria trays in upstate New York, East Coast surfer Dimitrije Milovich develops an alternative design based on surfboard technology, with a pressure-molded foam core wrapped in fiberglass, an extra-wide nose, channels in the base and a swallowtail. **1972** Milovich begins selling his boards under the name Winterstick. *Newsweek* and *Powder* take notice. **1977** Sims debuts its first production snowboard, the Flying Yellow Banana, made out of molded plastic with a wood Lonnie Toft skateboard deck on top. Early riders use Skyhook skateboard bindings or conventional ski bindings mounted mono-ski style. The same year, two other young tinkerers enter the fray: Mike Olsen, soon of Lib Tech and Mervin Manufacturing fame, and Jake Burton Carpenter (now Jake Burton), who moves to Vermont and gets serious about the Snurfer-inspired designs he's been experimenting with throughout the '70s. **1978** Chuck Barfoot, Sims and Weber cop some Winterstick ideas and create powder boards with fins and strap bindings. **1979** At the last Snurfer contest ever held, the first with national coverage and commercials, Burton shakes it up with his own custom design. Sponsored Snurfer pro and early organizer Paul Graves appears in a Labatt's Beer commercial, number one in two zillion snowboard ads to come. In Tahoe City, skater/riders christen the world's first snow half-pipe near the town dump. **1980** Burton Snowboards is founded. Both Burton and Winterstick experiment with ski technology like P-tex bases. **1982** Paul Graves organizes the National Snowsurfing Championships at Suicide Six Ski Area in Vermont, featuring slalom and downhill, where speeds in excess of 60 mph are reported. **1983** Burton puts on the National Snowboarding Championships at Snow Valley, VT. Tom Sims attends, then goes home to hold the inaugural World Snowboarding Championships near Lake Tahoe, the first contest ever to feature a half-pipe event. Considering it a travesty unworthy of inclusion in the overall title, the Burton team boycotts the half-pipe event. That season, the first highback bindings appear, enabling hard-pack riding. **1985** *Absolutely Radical* is the first exclusively snowboard magazine. Later changes its name to *International Snowboard*. Metal edges are introduced on Sims 1500 FE and Burton Performer models. Surfing-influenced fins are gone once and

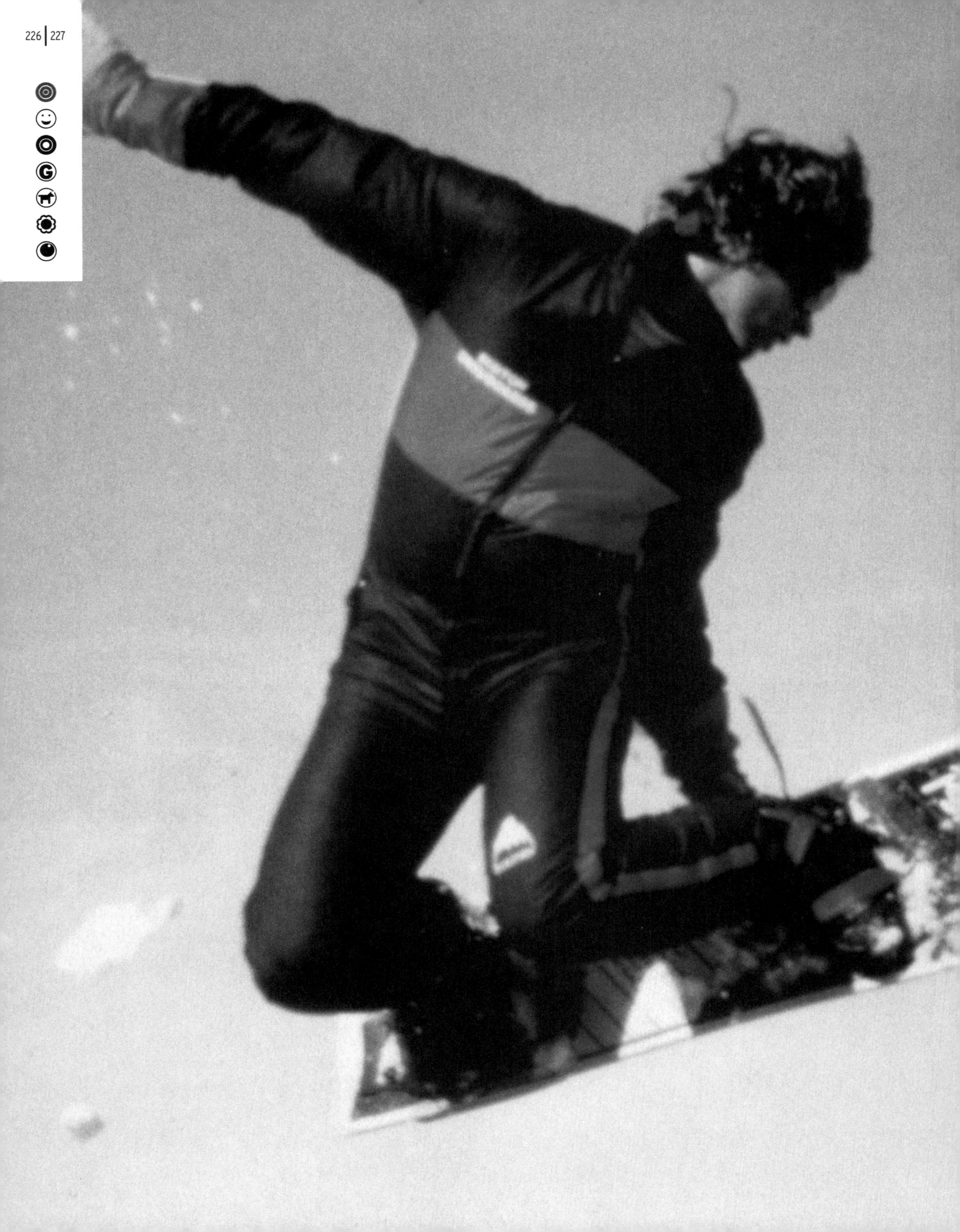

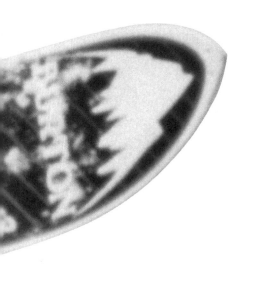

for all. First signature model appears, Sims's Terry Kidwell, the first freestyle board with a rounded tail. Mike Olsen's Gnu boards are marketed as the first carving boards. **1986** The Swiss Championships in St. Moritz mark the beginning of serious European snowboarding. Hooger Booger produces the first asymmetrical race board. The Worlds, meanwhile, switch to Breckenridge, CO, and lucrative Swatch sponsorship. Stratton Mountain, VT, is the first resort to offer snowboard lessons. **1987** Burton introduces a lace-up soft boot with a ski boot bladder, now the standard design. Barfoot makes the first twin-tip. *TransWorld SNOWboarding* begins publishing. **1988** Ocean Pacific leads a wave of surf industry players into the snowboard trade with a line of clothing. Burton defeats Sims in a court battle over who gets to sponsor Craig Kelly. Proving anyone can go big, Eddie "The Eagle" Edwards becomes the toast of the Calgary Olympics as Britain's lone ski jumper. Outfitted with equipment donated by other jumpers, the true amateur finishes a distant last. **1989** Major resorts like Squaw, Mammoth, Vail and Snowbird finally allow the one-plank barbarians past the gate. Rob Morrow forms Morrow Snowboards. **1990** Santa Cruz joins a growing list of skate/ snow industry crossovers. World's first snowboard park created at Val Ski Resort. **1993** The International Snowboard Federation hosts its first official World Champi- onships in Austria. Americans Kevin Delaney and Michele Taggart win the combined titles. *Blunt* debuts, pioneering video frame grabs and wild graphics that capture the attention of the snowboard industry, now some 50 manufacturers strong. *Snowboarder TV* debuts on ESPN with host Greg Tomlinson. Matt Goodwill and Greta Gaines win the first World Extreme Snowboard Championships in Valdez, AK. Negotiations begin that lead to a full-season World Cup and sanctioning by the super- bureaucratic Fédération International de Ski which yields, eventually, to the admission of snowboarding to the Olympic family at the '98 Nagano Games. **1994** Signs of the times: Ride becomes the first snowboard company to go public on the NASDAQ stock exchange, and Burton produces an interactive CD-ROM catalog. **1995** *Heckler* is the first snowboard magazine to publish on the World Wide Web. Five manufacturers introduce step-in bindings for soft boots. **1996** Roughly half of all sliders making their first visit to a ski resort are on snowboards, and one-third of them are female. **1997** Snowboarders are front-and-center at the inaugural Winter X Games in California. **1998** At Nagano, Canada's Ross Rebagliati wins the first snowboarding Olympic gold medal in giant slalom, then has it taken away for testing positive for marijuana. Blaming the trace levels on passive smoke from hanging with huffers, he turns Bill Clinton's excuse upside-down: he didn't partake, but he did inhale. Miraculously, they give the medal back. Snowboarding says it's sorry and will never, *ever* do it again.

229 229 229 229

SNOW IN SAN DIEGO

UNLIKE THE SHAVED ICE YOU MAY HAVE SEEN at other artificial snow jumps, San Diego's inaugural summer big air contest in '97 used the real thing. Sort of.

Here's how they did it: First, they built the ramp. Two hundred fifty feet long and 90 feet high, it used eight semi-trailer loads of scaffolding and 50,000 pounds of cement at the base. It took two days and tanker trucks filled with 60,000 gallons of liquid nitrogen and 60,000 gallons of good old H_2O to cover the ramp. Compressed air forced the super-cold nitrogen (-320° F) together with water out through two huge snow guns. Working from the top down, each gun was surrounded by a mobile tent to keep the snow falling on the ramp. After doing a base layer overnight, they covered it with insulating blankets. The morning of the contest, they topped up the snowpack to a respectable one foot, some 200 tons of San Diego pow-pow altogether. Despite a blazing sun that sent the temperature soaring, the huckers were able to soar along with it.

As you watch big air, you'll notice that sometimes the tricks are so new, or so altered from their known versions, that even expert commentators are at a loss to identify them by name. No deal—in fact, relentless innovation is a core value of snowboarding. But here are some standard tricks you'll see wherever riders gather on a snowy slope with a few shovels and a truckload of peer pressure.

CHICKEN SALAD AIR One of many standard grab options that spice up any kind of jump. Rear hand grasps the heel edge between the legs, with the wrist rotated inward to complete the grab. CORKSCREW Once riders have mastered spinning tricks in an upright posture, they'll start executing them horizontally in mid-air. CRAIL AIR Rear hand grabs toe edge in front of the front foot while the rear leg is boned. FRONTSIDE AIR A grab with the rear hand between the feet on the toe edge with the front leg boned. Also *Frontside Indy*. INDY AIR Performed backside with the rear hand grabbing toe edge between the bindings. INVERT A trick where the head is beneath the board at some point in the jump. JAPAN AIR Front hand grabs toe edge in front of the front foot. Both knees are bent, the rear leg is boned and the board is pulled to the level of the head. LIEN AIR Front hand grabs heel edge and the body leans out over the nose. MELONCHOLLIE AIR Front hand reaches behind the front leg and grabs heel edge while the front leg is boned. METHOD AIR The front hand grabs heel edge, both knees are bent and the board is pulled level to the head. MISTY FLIP The straight-jump version of half-pipe's McTwist, it's a partially inverted 540 Frontflip that goes from forward to fakie or vice versa. MUTE AIR Front hand grabs toe edge between or in front of the feet. NOLLIE FRONTFLIP A spring off the nose while going off a jump and doing a front somersault. NUCLEAR AIR The rear hand reaches across the front of the body and grabs the heels edge in front of the front foot. PALMER AIR Named after Shaun Palmer, it's a kind of Method Air where the grab is near the nose, the board is pulled across the front of the body and the nose is pointed downward. POP TART Airing from fakie to forward in the half-pipe without rotating. ROAST BEEF AIR Rear hand reaches between the legs and grabs the heel edge while the rear leg is boned. ROCKET AIR Front hand grabs toe edge in front of the front foot while the back leg is boned and the board is perpendicular to the ground. ROLLING DOWN THE WINDOWS When a rider is caught off balance and is fighting to stay upright with a wild rotation of the arms. SEATBELT The front hand reaches across the body and grabs the tail while the front leg is boned. SLOB AIR A Frontside Air where the front hand grabs mute, the back leg is boned and the board is kept parallel with the ground. SPAGHETTI AIR The front hand reaches between the legs to grab the toe edge in front of the front foot, while the back leg is boned. STALEFISH AIR A frontside trick where the rear hand grabs the heel edge between the bindings, but coming from behind the rear leg. STALEMASKY AIR Front hand reaches between the legs and grabs the heel edge while the front leg is boned. STIFFY AIR Any trick where both legs are boned and a grab is thrown in. TAIPAN AIR Front hand reaches behind the front foot, grabs toe edge between the bindings and the front knee is bent to touch the board, tuck-knee style.

SNOWBOARDING'S "GO BIG OR GO HOME"
mantra makes the big air discipline
the marquee event at many pro competitions. This is largely because it's a prime
time version of a scene that repeats
itself in resort areas and back hills
around the globe: a bunch of riders hanging around a big hit, pushing one another
to ever-sicker heights.

Going huge and clean is what big air is
all about. For that reason, riders have to
decide how technical they can get while
still assuring that they can stand it up.
Once settled on a trick, the rider then
has to introduce as many idiosyncratic
tweaks as possible in order to show
personal style. Grabs, bones, late moves,
off-axis spinning—snowboarders have a
complex array of style gestures whose
difficulty takes a lot of experience to
assess. Keep in mind, too, that although
the manmade snow of the San Diego ramp
made for a decent landing area, many of
the riskier jumps you see in videos can only
be safely attempted in the back country,
where deep powder will cushion a fall.

The X Games big air format is a simple
one. Each competitor gets three chances to
bust something earth-shaking—and only
the best score of the three counts. Five
judges each render a whole-number score
out of 100, composed of up to 25 for the
trick, up to 25 more for execution, and up
to 50 points for amplitude—both height and
distance. Of the five numbers, the highest
and lowest are thrown out, leaving the rest
to be averaged to two decimal points.

Snowboarding technology has come a long way in a short time, but as far as beginners are concerned, it matters little. As big air specialist Kevin Jones tells newbies, "The equipment can get quite expensive, but I recommend you buy your buddy's old board for, like, $100, then pick up some Sorels at a Price Club. An inexperienced rider won't be able to tell if the equipment is good or bad."

GOOD TO GO

Burton's Rippey 56s, designed by, you got it, Jim Rippey: $430 each. Custom Freestyle bindings: $169.95.

THERE ARE TWO APPROACHES TO SNOWBOARDING. One is with HARD BOOTS, a ski-boot equivalent that clips into PLATE BINDINGS. This is for riders who prefer a narrower RACING BOARD that's designed for carving heavy turns on groomed slopes. They generally have more of a forward-facing stance, and are hard to ride fakie. The second approach, favored in the half-pipe and for big air hits, is the SOFT BOOT setup. This can be paired with a TWIN-TIP FREESTYLE BOARD, or a directional ALL-MOUNTAIN FREERIDER. Most beginners also like the comfort and the adjustable straps of standard FREESTYLE BINDINGS Some soft-boot riders use a stance with their feet straight across the board, while others like them pointed slightly forward in the manner of a surfer. Beginners should always give some thought to their preferred stance before renting or buying—don't let a busy techie just ram the standard set-up down your throat. The latest innovation in soft-boot technology is a variety of STEP-IN BINDINGS like Switch and K2 Clicker. With mechanisms similar to the clipless pedals of mountain biking, they eliminate post-chairlift grovelling and offer a great deal of convenience. While riders have discovered that they are beefy enough to survive most on-mountain maneuvers, big air huckers still stick to the failproof freestyle setup. You can drop a lot of bank on fashion, but at the very least you'll need waterproof PANTS and good-quality GLOVES.

JIM RIPPEY Above the kicker, Rippey looks like a cat contorted in precarious positions. Part of the crew that elevated snowboarding to where it is today, he still returns solidly to earth.

PETER LINE Often copied but never outdone, Line is equally strong in the half-pipe and off of big air kickers. Small in stature, he can stomp Switch 900s and Corkscrews.

KEVIN JONES One of the big air masters, he's a born comedian, always smiling. Respected for making incredibly fluid spins both frontside and backside, he's known to bust out 720 or 900 Corkscrews to push the level one step further.

JASON BORGSTEDE Powerful and consistent, he developed from an all-mountain rider in Alaska to a big air hucker. Perfect execution of spinning grabs and Rodeo Flips, he can hang with the world's best.

BARRETT CHRISTY A complete all-mountain rider, she's one of the strongest women on a board today, known to go bigger than most guys. Her number one priority: Ride.

KEVIN JONES

GROWING UP IN CALIFORNIA, KEVIN JONES WAS A SKATEBOARDER who had a bone to pick with snowboarders. He thought they were wannabes who were ripping off the soul of skateboarding. But then he met a few cool snowboarders who turned him on to a classic vid called *Riders on the Storm*, and that was all he needed. He was hooked. "I thought I was going to be a rock star," says Jones, who once played bass in a funk band called Yukon Cornelius. "Then I went snowboarding. Funny how one day can change your life."

Jones now lives in Truckee, CA, with Jim Rippey and Jimmy Halopoff, and stars in films just like the one that got him started. He is also a big air specialist with numerous wins to his credit, although he had to settle for silver on the San Diego snow. Not that it wasn't fun: "Everyone was super amped," he says of the summer session. "People were grabbing at my clothes. Girls were asking me to sign their butts—I even gave my pants away." It's a good thing his only superstition is to buy new underwear before competitions.

"Contests just got good again," he notes. "They were pretty stupid up until about two years ago. The judging was so biased, and the half-pipes were ridiculously lame." But don't get him started about the money that's available. "Horrible," he says. "Europe is the place to go." Jones says the typical purse for first place at a European contest is around $50,000." By contrast, U.S. contests offer $10,000 for the top finisher, although the prize money does trickle down deeper through the field.

It's hard, though, to summon too much pity for a guy whose job description involves riding five or six days a week—including summers in New Zealand's Southern Alps. Oh, well, he can always quit the business and go back to an honest profession: there are still plenty of openings for rock stars.

PETER LINE

WITH A STRONG SKATEBOARD/SKIING BACKGROUND, Peter Line has earned a reputation as a fearless airman. And in a world where the laws aren't strict enough regarding kooks who hang around lodges spraying about their massive exploits, the Kirkland, WA, pro is a refreshing throwback to the strong, silent type. "When I do say something," he says, "the little gremlin who lives in my brain takes over what I'm saying and he's not quite able to put the words together like he would want, and they come out garbled and twisted." So Line keeps quiet. Video kingpin Michael "Mack Dawg" McEntire pays him the highest compliment when he says, "He lets his riding speak for itself." At X Games '97, it talked its way to big air gold.

Line is on the gremlin side himself, a birdlike five foot six, 130. But he's a bundle of controlled energy, permanently stoked about a job that involves stomping Switch 900s in contests and slashing Cascade powder for the camera. "It has gone beyond my wildest dreams," he says. "I got to travel all over the world, see all these crazy places, do something I love and make a living off it. I still haven't comprehended it all yet." Line recently got into business with fellow pro Ingemar Backman in a clothing company called Four Square. "I mostly snowboard just for the fun of it," he says, "but I like to do things on the business side too—something that makes me feel a little more worthwhile. People need to feel useful to be happy."

BARRETT CHRISTY

MANY SLIDERS DREAM OF SOME DAY RELOCATING to a Colorado mountain town and taking up The Life. Barrett Christy went the dream one better: the Vail resident has ridden her way to a position as one of snowboarding's top female pros. She hurled her way to gold at the first Winter X Games big air and slopestyle events in '97.

Originally a skier, Christy remembers, "My friends were snowboarding and I was frustrated because they were cruising by me, having all the fun." On her first one-plank day, she fell and broke her tailbone—although it wasn't diagnosed until four years later when a doctor told her a bit of bone was floating around in there. "Before that, people at school thought I was always just whining."

As well as she performs in a variety of disciplines, Christy has a bit of a love-hate relationship with competition. "You can't just get up the day before and rule." Besides, she adds, "competitions take you away from the rest of the mountain."

As long as she's having fun, though, she'll continue to enter events. She's increasing her fitness with weights, running, yoga and mountain biking, and once competed in wakeboarding. Also, in a bid to lower her caffeine intake, Christy guzzles algae supplements in the morning.

Her advice to hot young riders hoping to go pro: Do it for love, not money. "Don't try to get started just to get sponsored. If that's your only goal, it's not fun."

JIM RIPPEY

WHEREVER CLIFFS ARE DROPPED AND HUGE tricks stomped, riders owe a small debt to Jim Rippey. As part of the crew whose Alaska-sized exploits have been the centerpiece of some of snowboarding's most influential videos, Rippey raised the bar on what snowboarders consider big air. As an amateur, Rippey stayed pretty focused on competitions. But ever since he first saw the Burton team while working as a liftie at Donner Ski Ranch, he's had one thing in mind: "What job could be better than that?" Nowadays he spends most of his time filming in glamor locations around the world. He's the guy they count on for smooth, three-minute segments on big mountains and, of course, King Kong hucks. "I might do five or six 50-foot drops in a day. We're out there trying to get footage that has never been captured before."

Incredibly confident during high flight, Rippey has probably tried more trick variations in big air than any other rider. And he knows how to put on a show. At the '97 Winter X Games, Rippey heard at the top of the run that the program would be seen on *Wide World of Sports* and globally on ESPN International. He couldn't help but introduce some style into an event that is supposed to be about speed—he hucked a backflip over the water gap, jibbed off of Rob Kingwill's nose and still managed to make the finals.

SHELLY UECKERT

SHELLY UECKERT HAS A BIT OF FRIENDLY
advice: If your Mom tells you she knows you better than you know yourself, don't be so quick to brush her off. It seems Ueckert used to hate the snow and cold and thought skiing was a chore. In fact, after graduating from high school she moved to Florida hoping never to see it again. A few years later, however, her mother kept insisting that there was a sport tailor-made for her daughter. "She really wanted me to come back to Flagstaff and try snowboarding," says Ueckert. "She just knew that I would like it." Not only did she like it, she could tell on the first day that it was going to change her life.

Now living in San Diego, her roommate is a rat named Puppycat that, like its human, performs tricks on command. But Ueckert very nearly missed the '97 summer big air event because, as a part-time waitress, she needed someone to cover a lunch shift. "I think someone will help me out," she told reporters. "After all, this is the X Games." Once the personnel problems were sorted out, Ueckert busted her way to a third-place finish on the towering ramp.

"It's all in your head, the big air stuff," she notes. "You have to have everything planned out in your mind. You can't hesitate."

What about fear? A necessity, Ueckert says: "All the X Gamers are in it for the fear element."

STAY TUNED ICE CLIMBING FREE SKIING SKIBOARDING SNOCROSS SNOW MOUNTAIN BIKE RACING SNOWBOARDING

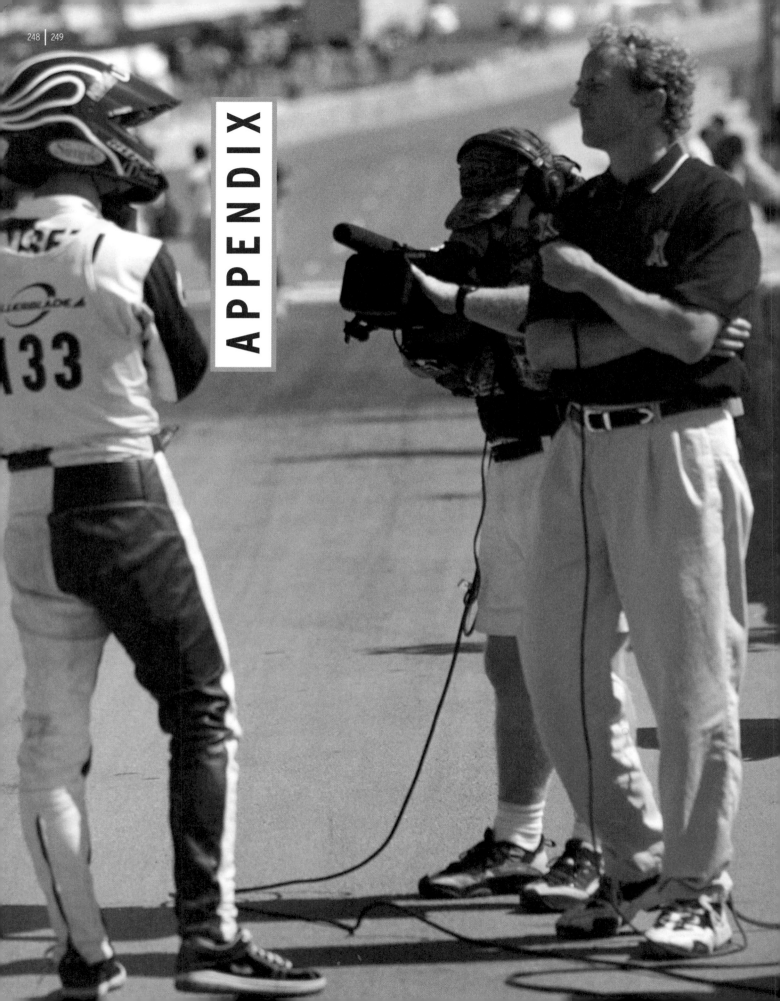

APPENDIX

X GAME RESULTS

AS INSIDE AS IT GETS
By Chris Fowler

ESPN's X Games television coverage began in Rhode Island back in 1995 with a confession: we weren't sure what to expect. Not even weeks spent chewing through a 20-pound research manual prepared us to prepare curious viewers for whatever strange stuff might unfold.

Decaying Fort Adams, built to protect Newport Harbor from the British, had been invaded by an army of extremists, the world's best in sports that most of the world never knew existed. Just outside the fort's walls in the dusty TV compound, I remember there was a great sense of anticipation, mixed with the usual big-event anxiety.

I also remember there was no indoor plumbing. Thanks to a handpicked team of ESPN production all-stars, this would be world-class television . . . produced in third-world comfort.

Television critics mostly bashed the X Games' concept. One wrote that my assignment as co-host meant that I must have drawn "the short straw." That notion was dead wrong, but I still wondered if having street luge on the resume would help my career. Security came from knowing I was going into this weird new world along with the best TV types I'd ever worked with.

The partnership between corporate television and rebel athletes was a little tense. An in-line skater was asked to pose for a routine "head shot." He was asked to hold up a slate with his name on it. And to remove his baseball hat. And, if that wasn't too much trouble, could he look at the camera? He shook his head with disgust, smirking, "Too many rules, dude."

But once the '95 Games began, we realized we were on to something. You didn't have to know everything about skateboarding to appreciate the awesome skill of Tony Hawk. Watching Matt Hoffman rise to the moment—his bike soaring into the black sky above the half-pipe as a thousand fans roared—was a rush of contagious adrenaline that caught us neophytes off guard. Plus, a street luge smashing into a hay bale—when seen from the racer's helmet-cam—is the kind of good, clean fun that makes compelling TV.

During our nightly shows, a cold, thick New England fog would roll in. From the set, we had a hazy view of the venues, fans wandering the dusty field—with the tunes pounding from speaker stacks the scene resembled a mini-Lollapalooza. I've snowshoed in the Rockies and climbed high in the Himalayas, but I've never been colder than I was on those June Newport nights, wearing five layers and waiting for the broadcast to end.

But how could we whine? There were teams of sleep-deprived adventure racers getting dunked in icy rapids, wading through leech-infested swamps, navigating toward Fort Adams and loving every bit of it. For them, the only worthwhile challenge is one that pushes their minds and bodies to the brink. If you think it's corny to call the X Games inspiring, well, you had to be there . . . to see five exhausted, tearful Aussies paddle ashore after a five-day odyssey. Or watch 85-pound Katie Brown assert her genius on the vertical chessboard of the climbing wall. Or the late Rob Harris's inverted spin while plummeting two miles per minute on his skysurfboard.

Do the X Games represent sports in a pure form? Nope. We've found in the years since we lauched them that alternative athletes can dish out as much attitude and ego as any professional superstar. There's plenty of politics and controversy. Some showboating to seduce sponsors, who too often rule the day. But it's worth it.

The X Games might never amount to a true revolution, maybe just a welcome diversion on the crowded sports calendar. But if you arrive with an open mind, you'll get sucked in. The energy is contagious.

Even if we're *still* not certain exactly what to expect.

STREET LUGE (CONT'D)

SUPER MASS		
	1	Chris Ponseti
	2	Biker Sherlock
	3	Rat Sult

DUAL		
	1	Biker Sherlock
	2	Dennis Derammelaere
	3	Darren Lott

1996
MASS
1 Biker Sherlock
2 Daryl Thompson
3 Dennis Derammelaere

DUAL
1 Shawn Goulart
2 Stefan Wagner
3 Dennis Derammelaere

1995
MASS
1 Shawn Goulart
2 Lee Dansie
3 Stefan Wagner

DUAL
1 Bob Pereyra
2 Stefan Wagner
3 Shawn Goulart

WAKEBOARDING

1997
MEN'S
1 Jeremy Kovac
2 Darin Shapiro
3 Parks Bonifay

WOMEN'S
1 Tara Hamilton
2 Andrea Gaytan
3 Jaime Necrason

1996
COED
1 Parks Bonifay
2 Jeremy Kovac
3 Scott Byerly

BAREFOOT JUMPING

1997
1 Peter Fleck
2 Evan Berger
3 Warren Fine

1996
1 Ron Scarpa
2 Jon Kretchman
3 Rael Nurick

1995
1 Justin Seers
2 Ron Scarpa
3 Rael Nurick

BICYCLE STUNT

1997
VERT
1 Dave Mirra
2 Dennis McCoy
3 Matt Hoffman

STREET
1 Dave Mirra
2 Dennis McCoy
3 Dave Voelker

DIRT
1 T.J. Lavin
2 Brian Foster
3 Ryan Nyquist

FLATLAND
1 Trevor Meyer
2 Nate Hanson
3 Andrew Faris

CANDID CAMERAS

Over 100 camera positions are used to cover the X Games, including more than 30 point-of-view (POV) cameras:

STREET LUGE / DOWNHILL IN-LINE

OVERHEAD ROBOTIC CAMERAS **are suspended over a pivotal turn and the finish line in the street luge and down-hill in-line courses.** POLE-CAMS **are miniature-lensed cameras attached to the end of poles held over the hay bales lining the courses to provide low-level speed shots. These supplement the** COURSE-CAMS, **which are mini cameras situated throughout the entire course to capture speed shots. Street luge utilizes** LUGE-CAMS, **mounted directly on the sled, to enhance the viewer's perspective by traveling at 60 mph just inches off the ground. One mini-camera is on the bottom front of the sled, providing a ground level view, while another one is mounted to the top of the sled, point-ing at the pilot and the course ahead.**

SKYSURFING

Skysurfing has its own specific camera equipment involving HELMET-CAMS, **digital cameras attached to the helmet of the camera flyer and to an additional ESPN camera person who jumps along with the teams.** EXIT-CAMS **are three** POV **cameras carefully positioned near the exit of the plane.** IN-PLANE CAMERAS **capture the adrenaline building before the jumps are made.**

BICYCLE STUNT (CONT'D)

1996
VERT
1 Matt Hoffman
2 Dave Mirra
3 Jamie Bestwick

STREET
1 Dave Mirra
2 Jay Miron
3 Rob Nolli

DIRT
1 Joey Garcia
2 T.J. Lavin
3 Brian Foster

1995
VERT
1 Matt Hoffman
2 Dave Mirra
3 Jay Miron

DIRT
1 Jay Miron
2 Taj Mihelich
3 Joey Garcia

SPORTCLIMBING

1997
MEN'S
DIFFICULTY
1 Francois Legrand
2 Yuji Hirayama
3 Chris Sharma

WOMEN'S
DIFFICULTY
1 Katie Brown
2 Liv Sansoz
3 Muriel Sarkany

MEN'S
SPEED
1 Hans Florine
2 Chris Bloch
3 Jason Campbell

WOMEN'S
SPEED
1 Elena Ovtchinnikova
2 Abby Watkins
3 Mi-Sun Go

1996
MEN'S
DIFFICULTY
1 Arnaud Petit
2 Francois Lombard
3 Christian Brenna

WOMEN'S
DIFFICULTY
1 Katie Brown
2 Laurence Guyon
3 Liv Sansoz

MEN'S
SPEED
1 Hans Florine
2 Chris Bloch
3 Tim Fairfield

WOMEN'S
SPEED
1 Cecile Le Flem
2 Elena Shumilova
3 Natalie Richer

1995
MEN'S
DIFFICULTY
1 Ian Vickers
2 Arnaud Petit
3 Francois Petit

WOMEN'S
DIFFICULTY
1 Robyn Erbesfield
2 Elena Ovtchinnikova
3 Mia Axon

MEN'S
SPEED
1 Hans Florine
2 Salavat Rakhmetov
3 Yuji Hirayama

WOMEN'S
SPEED
1 Elena Ovtchinnikova
2 Diane Russell
3 Georgia Phipps-Franklin

BIG AIR SNOWBOARDING

SUMMER

1997 MEN	1	Peter Line
	2	Kevin Jones
	3	Jason Borgstede

WOMEN	1	Tina Dixon
	2	Hillary Maybery
	3	Shelly Ueckert

EXTREME ADVENTURE RACE

1997	1	Team Presidio
	2	Team Endeavor
	3	Team Red Hot

1996	1	Team Thredbo
	2	Twin Team
	3	Team Eco-Internet

ECO-CHALLENGE

1995	1	Team Kobeer
	2	Team Eco-Internet
	3	Team Mirage

BUNGEE JUMPING

1996	1	Peter Bihun
	2	Doug Anderson
	3	Carolyn Anderson

1995	1	Doug Anderson
	2	Mark Baldwin
	3	Todd Watkins

WATER SPORTS

Water sports rely on a ROPE-CAM, a miniature RF (radio frequency) camera located on the handle of the rope to get closeups of the competitors. Two JUMP-CAMS are situated on the ramp in barefoot jumping.

AGGRESSIVE IN-LINE/BICYCLE STUNT/SKATEBOARDING/SPORT-CLIMBING/BIG AIR SNOWBOARDING

A super slo-mo CRANE-ROBOTIC CAMERA sits atop a crane designed to capture Vert and big air competitors at the apex of their jumps. The crane can drop 85 feet in eight seconds. The CABLE-CAM moves robotically across a 1,200-foot span of cable positioned over the entire X Games arena, while WALL-CAMS are placed at the top of the sportclimbing walls and along the bike and in-line Street courses.

ACKNOWLEDGMENTS

Above all, my gratitude to everyone associated with ESPN and the X Games in Bristol, New York and San Diego who contributed their time, enthusiasm and Xpertise. You are simply the best.

The X Games are run by a terrific group of people, without whom this book would not have been possible—or as much fun to produce. Chris Stiepock and Amy Cacciola were instrumental from start to finish, and loaned out their secret weapon, Ian Votteri, to write the athlete mini-profiles. Chris Fowler took us expertly behind the scenes. The following X Games executives and insiders gave the book a much appreciated final read: Tom Clendenin, Rich Feinberg, Fred Gaudelli, Dick Glover, Josh Krulewitz, Jeff Ruhe and Ron Semiao. I owe a special debt to John Walsh for setting the overall standards so high. Eric Schoenfeld kept me checked and balanced. Sharyn Taymor kept the trains running at full speed. Kil-Jae Hong kept the book in the spotlight. Julie Cianci kept everyone well copied.

Much of the information in the book came from the exhaustive in-house research manuals prepared by Deborah McKinnis and her crew. A special thank you to Deb, Stuart Hothem, Edward Marshall and researchers Ryn Reid (skateboarding), Sam Bridgham (skysurfing), David Dobson (downhill in-line and street luge), Eileen Hansen (aggressive in-line), Dean Turcol (water sports), Bridget Quinn (bicycle stunt and sportclimbing) and Kathy Gutowski (flatland and big air snowboarding). We are also indebted to sport organizers Pete McKeeman (skysurfing), Steve Novak (downhill in-line), Mark Shays (aggressive in-line), Marcus Rietema (street luge), Dean Turcol (water sports), Matt Hoffman (bicycle stunt), Jim Wah (sportclimbing) and Danielle and Dan Bostick (big air snowboarding and skateboarding) and judges Jeffrey Serrault (skysurfing), Nikki Lee (wakeboarding), Sam Spano (barefoot jumping), Mark Losey and Steve Buddendeck (bicycle stunt).

Scott Clarke, Eric Lars Bakke and Dana Paul have been documenting the X Games since 1995. No one gets more inside or returns with better action photographs. We're also grateful to the following for contributing additional action and equipment photographs: Tanya Hyder (Sun Path Products, Inc.), Mark Sanders (Roces USA), Rollerblade, Inc., Jim Reidy (Full Tilt), Hyperlite, Tony Teske (HO Sports), Robert Castillo (GT Bicycles), Bryan Baxter (Hoffman Bikes), Dr. Peter J. Barrett, Wolfgang Schweiger (PMI/Petzl Dist.) and Brian Martin and Barry Dugan (Burton Snowboards).

Last July, agent Laura Hinds introduced me to photographer Michael Wong, for whom the look and lifestyle of extreme sports are as natural as breathing. He turned out to be that rare combination of artist and really nice guy—and the missing link to making a good book great. Our gratitude to the following people and companies for helping to make his shots come alive: Matt Hensley, Alphonzo Rawls, Lance Conkin, Dave Andrecht (Duff Shoes), Julie Brandt, Verducci In-Line Skates, Lucci Giordano, Sergio Dantas, Biker Sherlock, Dregs Skateboards, Ben Lewis, Corey Marotta, Aaron Grace, Michael Lord, Tally Kuhl, Stinger Wakeboards, SMP Clothing, Black Fly Eyewear, Rusty Wakeboards and Eric Monteleone.

At Hyperion, Gretchen Young's commitment to creativity and quality is a continual gift. Jennifer Morgan was a source of consistent support and enthusiasm for the project. Linda Prather's calm commitment to excellence took the production and printing of the book to another level. Thanks also to David Lott and John Marius for taking such care with the manuscript and cover, Laurie Rippon and Tracey Menzies for marketing the book with style and Robert Miller and Kris Kliemann for their ongoing support.

Hadas Dembo brought taste and charm to the photo research and editing, while Helene Silverman brought sophistication and intelligence to the art direction. Felicity Stone kept her cool—and her sense of humor—as she navigated us through the maddeningly inconsistent world of extreme-speak. Andrew Giammarco stepped in to make the production process run as smoothly as he does. Monica Schroer helped get the ball (or should that be "skateboard") rolling. Jenny Ford did it all with grace and style—from editorial research to photo research, from production to fact-checking, from writing to more scanning, photocopying and collating in two months than any human being should have to do in a lifetime.

Finally, I can't thank Kevin Brooker enough for giving the book its voice and Heidi Fener enough for giving the book its look. Uniquely special talents, they're the best creative partners I could have asked for.

Shelley Youngblut, Editorial Director